Occasional Papers:
Teaching Writing in a Way That Students Embrace Enthusiastically

by:

Bill Martin and Christine Gorychka

Purple Feather Press

BOOKS AND CREATIVE PUBLISHING

Title: Occasional Papers: Teaching Writing in a Way That Students Embrace
Enthusiastically

Printed in the United States of America
First Printing April 2025

ISBN 978-1-959600-09-1

Purple Feather Press
Georgetown, TX 78628
www.PurpleFeatherPress.com

Table of Contents

Structure of the Chapters

Readers will find these elements in each chapter:

Where are you now as a teacher of writing? Reflective questions pertaining to the chapter ask readers to respond with their ideas, keeping in mind their current writing instruction.

What we do. This section provides background information about Occasional Papers (OPs), including supportive research, and emphasizes how OPs can be the basis for writing instruction.

Different ways to get there. Readers learn about the various aspects of using Occasional Papers in their classrooms, and how flexible implementation can be.

Your Turn. In this section readers sketch out a lesson idea in order to complete a suggested activity.

Reflections. Readers reflect about what they have read and the activity they have completed. (We anticipate possible questions, and we will include a Q and A on how to deal with those questions.)

Personal Reflection. Some of the chapters will include a short story, a testimony, a Q and A, etc. that supports the chapter's premise.

Works Cited. Some chapters will include a bibliography of works cited by the authors.

Resources. This section includes additional activities and teacher support.

Acknowledgement

We thank Dr. Kay Psencik (Senior Consultant, Learning Forward) for embracing our ideas about Occasional Papers, supporting the impact they can have for teachers and their students, and then guiding us in building a framework for our book.

Chapter Summaries

Chapter One – What Is an Occasional Paper? What Makes an Occasional Paper Different?

In this chapter we share the story of how Occasional Papers began. We explain the essential aspects of the program: motivation, authentic audiences, response to content, power of agenda, and respect and appreciation, and how these essentials are demonstrated in Occasional Papers (OPs). We end the chapter with a discussion of additional essential structures including manuscript expectations, grading, scheduling, and topic focus.

Chapter Two – Getting Ready: Introduction to the OP Rhythm

In this chapter we lead teachers through the "recipe" they must follow in order to explain to students what an Occasional Paper or OP is and how to write one. The recipe includes the following steps:
1. Look out for a moment that makes you stop and think.
2. Describe the moment.
3. Reflect (in writing) on its significance.
4. Read your OP aloud to an audience.
5. Respond to audience questions about content.
6. Write an author's note on your writing and the discussion.

This chapter also includes introductory activities teachers can use as they lead their students through the Occasional Paper recipe.

Chapter Three – First Attempt: The Real OP Procedure

With a series of steps, we look closely at what goes into the writing of Occasional Papers in a normal classroom setting. Even though the OP recipe is simple and the introductory activities can be helpful, students will at first have an incomplete picture of this process. We think the best place to begin is with topic selection and examples of what students can write about or what we call "OP moments." After identifying a topic, the next step is a written description. We provide teachers with samples of developed descriptions of experiences and advise them to encourage their students to describe their experiences with as much detail as possible. Even though there is no formula for reflective thought, in our next step we explain through examples and inquiry techniques how teachers can teach or encourage reflection. The last step is revision, and although we don't require it, teachers should encourage their students to read their OPs aloud to themselves before they read them aloud to their classmates. Students usually discover needed revisions in content details and manuscript correctness.

Chapter Four – Inquiry-Based Discussion: To Unpack, To Reconsider, To Discover

We know students have valuable things to say, and we have found they will want a discussion to work if they are interested in what is being discussed. And, if students can discuss the content of OPs, that interest in discussion will transfer to the discussion of other types of writing. In this chapter we present a series of questions and comments that do not anticipate all the differing aspects of various situations. Nor do they take into account differing temperaments and differing teaching styles of individual teachers, yet these questions are a starting point for developing a practice with confidence. This chapter also includes many strategies a teacher can use to initiate discussions, redirect discussions, and elevate discussions to a more intellectual frame.

Chapter Five – Skills Without Drills

There are many ways of teaching skills without drills, but two things are almost always required. There must be models – not necessarily sentences or text presented as models but language that is used well, that you notice either in what you read or what you hear being read by others. There must also be models of writing that care about both the content and about the audience. Finally, there must be practice in using the stylistic choices in the right places. This means writing – and focusing on presentation rather than content for a change.

Chapter Six – Two Weeks of Occasional Papers in a Twelfth-Grade Classroom

One co-author kept notes on Occasional Paper activity during a two-week segment of his twelfth-grade English class. By this time in the grading period, he had introduced OPs, read a model he had written, and had students read "practice OPs" in groups. This chapter includes some of his comments, questions, and reflections on the reading and discussion of Occasional Papers. Additional questions or comments our readers may have about Occasional Papers are highlighted in Q&A text boxes throughout this chapter.

Chapter Seven – The Real Deal: Experience, Reflection, and Revision

Students can find reflecting about their experiences difficult because they often think their experiences are not significant or meaningful. Therefore, we have to demonstrate to them and practice with them how to find meaning in their experiences through written reflection, especially reflection that goes beyond cliche. We intend to help teachers work toward a classroom in which students see all the easy answers--all the easy ways to explain or respond to texts that are problematic and worth questioning. This chapter also provides strategies teachers can use to increase student self-awareness and metacognition.

Chapter Eight – Stress-Free Grading

This chapter describes how to include Occasional Papers in a traditional curriculum. We begin by explaining how grading OPs worked in our classrooms. In addition to a standard scope and sequence, we assigned a required number of Occasional Papers at the beginning of each grading period, usually two. Because students read their OPs aloud in class, they did not hand them in to us for marking; instead, we gave students credit for writing and reading their OPs aloud before a deadline. In this chapter we will also discuss possibilities for the presentation of OPs as formal papers, and self-evaluation methods for discussion. Our belief is writing is motivated by response, not evaluation. We have developed ways to give OPs credit without diluting the power of communication as the motivating force.

Chapter Nine – And Not Only That

We end our book by encouraging our readers not to give up, but to give Occasional Papers a try with their students. Teachers will be surprised by the flexibility in assigning OPs and the relief of not having piles of papers to mark. Occasional Papers become more than a writing exercise and even more than a way to learn about inquiry. They become a different way to go about self-education and a different way of experiencing life itself. This is engaged pedagogy, and it does not mean an abandonment of the traditional goals of academic work. But it does mean always thinking of traditional goals as markers or a bridge or a trail toward larger goals; "an unexamined life is not worth living" and all of that.

How to Use This Book

This book is designed to share with teachers how to implement Occasional Papers in their curriculums. OPs are a doorway to what authentic pieces of writing can offer: true communication. Students are not just writing for practice. They are not just writing for demonstration. They are not just writing for self-expression. They are not in any sense just writing for school. They are writing for real.

Below are ten reasons why teachers should include Occasional Papers in their writing instruction.

Impact	Occasional Papers invite students to claim agency, starting with affecting the minds of other students face-to-face and leading to eventually going out and doing some public writing which leads to changing the world. The effects of OPs are both external and internal. There is an internal focus on reflection and clarifying of the writer's own attitude and opinions, and an external focus on affecting and changing the audience. Writing can in this way change not only the writer but also the world.
Motivation	Writing to do something is more motivating than writing to earn a grade. Occasional Papers enable a teacher to motivate a great deal of writing without the burden of written comments and grading. OPs provide a perfect opportunity for students to take risks with ways of writing that might or might not work. In this sense OPs are more than a lively accessory to the more serious writing curriculum; they are a backbone by which the rest of the writing curriculum is supported.
Content	Occasional Papers shift the focus of students' writing experience from presentation of content to delivery of content. Delivery of content is the reason to do any real writing. Presentation plays a part in delivery, but the pay-off should be in the experience of content being received. That is the pay-off for the writer: to be understood by a reader and for that understanding to have made a difference. Real writing does real work in the world. To be a writer and to produce real writing that does that work will lead to better writing, and that means attention on the part of the writer to better presentation.

Teacher Tedium	Occasional Papers give students feedback in relation to the communication achieved by their writing. Teachers will sponsor writing and motivate writing without having to respond by making comments which are not only time consuming but of dubious value. Students seldom modify their writing behavior as the result of reading the comments made on their papers. In addition, the comments are often misunderstood and are just as often misguided because the comments are written not from the perspective of a reader but from the perspective of an evaluator.
Community	Students can actually test out their Occasional Papers with a real audience to see whether what they write will have the effect they want it to have. They can see and hear and even feel the success in the moment. OPs build a community in the classroom and force students to know each other, to speak to each other, and almost certainly to understand each other better. Students will learn more, risk more, and both succeed and even fail more, but thereby grow more as writers in a context of trust and confidence.
Civil Discourse	Occasional Papers teach students respect for others and how to listen and how to talk. Civil discourse is a goal of education or at least should be. We should strive to teach values of respect for differences of opinion and disagreement about how to put facts in a meaningful context. OPs give teachers a chance to teach these values by living them rather than simply by preaching them. At their best, OPs expose us to each other in uncomfortably honest ways. At our best, we respond to such OPs with respect and civility, with reason and concern.
Connected Curriculum	Occasional Papers connect the classroom with the outside world. Students may wonder what the content of school instruction has to do with normal, everyday life outside the classroom. OPs bring the concerns, problems, obsessions, and trivial observations of non-classroom life into the classroom conversation, and through that conversation ensure that life outside is given serious consideration.
Analysis and Synthesis	Occasional Papers teach students analysis and synthesis. OPs challenge them to look closely at what they think and how they respond and to ask themselves why they think or respond this way. Thinking hard is the core of analysis. OPs also encourage synthesis in finding commonalities in similar cases. In other words, OP's encourage careful and productive thinking.

Attitude	Occasional Papers will change the way students think about writing. Instead of seeing writing as a trap that will catch them and make them suffer for mistakes and oversights, students have opportunities to be known and to be heard on issues and concerns that are important in real life. When students are allowed to be known for who they are in the classroom and are given the power to set the agenda to a certain extent during a prescribed part of the class period, they will be more willing to participate in activities over which they have no power of agenda setting namely most of the mandatory curriculum.

Teachable Moments	Occasional Papers charge the atmosphere with teachable moments. Too often success in teaching is measured by the number of objectives addressed instead of being measured by the number of teachable moments recognized and actively embraced. OPs make a teacher's job both more difficult and more joyful. It is difficult to be "off script," to need to teach "on the fly," to grab the teachable moments as they come. But it also brings with the exhaustion a reward. It is for such moments that most of us are teachers. OPs bring us more of these moments.

Chapter One

What Is an Occasional Paper?
What Makes an Occasional Paper Different?

Where are you now as a teacher of writing?

1. How important is it for students to have a chance to write what they think about?

_____

2. What makes writing valuable and fun for students?

_____

3. What sorts of feedback are most likely to actually change student writing for the better?

_____

4. What kind of audience is ideal for students to share their writing?

_____

✍ ✍

What we do:

What is an Occasional Paper?
Every day, even before we eat breakfast, several things happen to us that could make us stop and think. We don't, however, spend much time actually thinking about them because we go on to other things we have to get done. Even less frequently do we write about these moments. What would be the point?

There is no one we are writing for, and anyway we are talking about seemingly inconsequential topics: *I forgot to get bread and cannot make toast. The coffee grounds smell good as I open the bag to spoon them into the coffee maker. Should I make the bed or not? I'll decide later.* Our days are full of these small seemingly inconsequential occurrences that we do not take the time to write about or even to think through their implications, to tease out the possible meanings we can bring to them. We do not explore the value of a morning routine that includes making the bed. We do not wonder about why an unmade bed is not troubling to us. It does not occur to us to interrogate the avoidance in relation to growing up with chores and responsibilities, and finally being in a position to make our own choices about making the bed.

There are many experiences like this that happen every day. We have plenty of topics for writing, but we have no motivation to do the writing. We do not have an audience, and we cannot convince ourselves to write simply for our own intellectual enrichment. Even though we may be convinced that such exploratory writing would benefit both our writing and our thinking, we just don't do it.

And yet these are the topics – the type of topics – that we ask our students to write about. This is the sort of writing around which we have developed our writing program. There are several reasons we think this type of writing is good to use as a basis for writing instruction. These are the topics that students can write about with authority. It is their experience. It is their life. They know what they are talking about better than anyone else. They are writing not so they can demonstrate mastery of some "schoolified" topic that the audience may know more about than they do. They are writing to communicate to an audience something the audience does not know. We guarantee our students an audience because they read their papers to their class – much like an "author's chair" activity.

Because the author is an authority, the class feels free to ask questions and the author probably loves this. Everyone enjoys talking about what they really know to an audience that is actually curious. We make sure that there is a content-based discussion rather than a stylistic critique following each paper. The content is what is communicated, and it is the communication that is important. The feedback students get is immediate, and it is based on the content.

What questions are there? What is unclear? What are the reasons for the positions or ideas? These questions make students aware of whether the paper impacts the audience in the intended way. Does the writing do what the author wants it to do? Student writers become more and more audience-conscious as they write more and hear more responses to their writing. The fact that students are writing a great deal and enjoying it also has a beneficial effect on their skills. Finally, they are writing about something they care about for an audience that cares about (or at least knows) them.

We call these papers OPs, short for Occasional Papers. These papers are the "backbone" of our writing instruction. Students write several during the grading period. They are what Arthur Applebee calls natural context writing, writing that does what writers want writing naturally to do – to communicate. Writers communicating with an audience is the natural context of writing. Do these Occasional Papers replace everything that we are used to teaching in a writing course: matters of correctness, expectations of genres, adjustments for different audiences, research considerations? No. The Occasional Papers do not, cannot, replace everything in a comprehensive writing curriculum. They are a backbone activity, an ongoing activity done over and over as a classroom routine that moves students toward thinking like writers and justifies them in thinking of themselves as writers.

The format of the paper is simple. An Occasional Paper is a two-part personal essay that begins with a description of an experience followed by a reflection about what made this experience important or what made it "worth thinking about." The essay itself is only one aspect of the assignment. It is also important for students to write about topics they care about and write about them when they feel moved to write. Students have freedom to choose anything that happened to them that made them think. Students also control the timing of the writing; they write when they have experiences they want to write about. They read their OP aloud to the class from a written copy, and they engage in content-based talk after reading their papers to their classmates.

When introducing Occasional Papers in the classroom, we begin with a teacher-written OP and then present to students what we call the OP recipe:

▶ Be on the lookout for a moment or an experience that makes you stop and think.

▶ Describe the moment or experience in writing.

▶ Add a reflection about its significance. Why does it matter to you?

▶ Read your OP aloud to an audience, probably a small group or our entire class.

▶ Respond to audience questions and comments about the content of your OP.

What effect does this have on student writing?

◆ Writing about our personal experiences leads us to understand we have important things to share with others.

◆ Writing about what we care about increases our interest in writing.

◆ When we write about what we care about, we are more likely to spend time ensuring the piece communicates what we want it to communicate.

◆ Having others reflect on our OP writing, challenges our thinking about the experience and adds opportunities to elaborate.

Different ways to get there:

What makes Occasional Papers different?

Students who write OPs *change* the quality of their writing for the better in the short-term over the course of a semester. However, the real benefit of OPs is their long-term effect. Occasional Papers make students' writing better in the long run just by virtue of making students see themselves as writers who will continue to write and continue to care about their writing. It is in the long-term benefits of OPs that we have the most faith and feel the case for OPs is the strongest.

If a conference or a series of lessons in argument can tighten and refine a student's paper, that is a short-term success. It is a success that we should work toward and celebrate. But if that student finds writing onerous and wants whenever possible to avoid it, the success has improved the paper but not the writer.

If, on the other hand, the conference or series of lessons opens the student to a new idea that she can use in her writing and she has writing opportunities, including future OPs, to practice and experiment with this new idea, then we are much more likely to be able to say this student has become a better writer. OPs provide this type of writing opportunity.

They are a doorway to what writing can offer: true communication. It is because of the following three unique aspects of Occasional Papers - topic choice, motivation for writing, and method of presentation - that they build a long-term basis for writing.

1. <u>Students writing OPs have the freedom to choose topics and temporarily set the agenda for the class discussion.</u>

Because the topics are experiences from their lives, no one can choose the topics for the students since no one has had their experiences. Students forced to write about other people's topics disconnects the students from the lived-through reality of their individual experiences, and this results in them not having anything they really want to say. When students choose topics from individual experiences, their writing is more thoughtful and engaging because they have something to say.

Finally, when students confront these real-life topics as content for their writing and thinking and also as the subject matter of their discussions, they see the content of their OPs as something to explore. Paulo Freire writes that "as they are increasingly posed with problems relating to themselves in the world . . . [students] will feel increasingly challenged and obliged to respond to that challenge" (81). Students who begin to question what they previously took for granted as true will start to feel a new sense of agency and power, feeling they are in charge of what they are saying. Students choosing their own topics and then writing about their experiences, reflecting about their experiences, reading their writing aloud, and finally discussing their writing with their classmates is a far richer assignment than writing about teacher-assigned topics.

At a presentation in Nashville, a man in the back of the room asked in a smug challenge, "How is this going to help them write about *Henderson, the Rain King*?" Certainly, there are ways in which papers about football are not as rich a challenge. But for a student who cares deeply about football, it can be a real and an important challenge to write about his experience and reflect about that experience. In a paper about football, a student has a reason for, a stake in, pursuing the ideas; he may not have the same motivation to write about Bellow's novel.

Because of the confidence students gain through writing Occasional Papers, they find teacher-assigned personal essays, literary analysis, and research less overwhelming and more engaging; students who write well about experiences with football, will write well about history, literature, or economics. These students become real writers.

2. <u>Students writing OPs read to other students who are interested in what they have to say.</u>

Students read their papers to an audience that responds immediately and an audience that matters to the author. Applebee reported in 1981 that the teacher was the primary audience for 88 percent of the student papers in his study (47). There is no reason to think that teacher behavior has changed in the intervening years.

Teachers may try to create the illusion of writing for a different audience through statements in the assignment such as "write as if you are reporting to the school board" or "pretend you are submitting a letter to the editor." These are, however, weak fantasies; few students can fool themselves into thinking it is not the teacher who is going to read, respond to, and grade the paper.

In the case of Occasional Papers, the audience is the class (including the teacher but not "teacher as evaluator"). This audience of valued peers motivates communication, and it also provides response which is a potent way for an author to gauge writing success. According to Dewey, an activity that does not include a consideration of consequences leads nowhere intellectually (Experience 87).

The consequences in this case are answers to questions such as these: Did the class enjoy my writing? Did the class understand my ideas? Did the class need more information or explanation? Did the class think my ideas were important? Did the class laugh at the funny parts?

3. <u>Students who write OPs have the benefit of hearing other ideas about what they have written.</u>

In *Dialogic Inquiry: Towards a Socio-cultural Practice and Theory of Education*, Gordon Wells says that the content of the paper becomes the topic of inquiry. In either a large class or small group setting, students listen to and then discuss the content of Occasional Papers. Since the papers are read aloud by the author, all surface level concerns (spelling, punctuation, capitalization, and presentation) are invisible. The audience is hearing the paper, not reading it off the page.

At the beginning of the semester, teachers can encourage the audience to ask questions. "What did you mean when you said this or that?" "Can you say more about this or that?" "Do you feel different about this or that now?" Eventually the class should be able to discuss OPs with little or no teacher prompting.

How do you write an Occasional Paper?
We think it is essential to explain to students what Occasional Papers are. (Actually, we introduce OPs with this text. We read it aloud to students as they follow on a hand-out. You may choose to introduce OPs in a different way.)

> Occasional papers (or OPs) are short papers written about an experience you had recently. An OP could be written about something that happened or something you read or heard about someone else's experience or an idea you have or had that is important to you. It could be pretty much anything that you experienced, that you feel is worth thinking about, and about which you have something to say.

> It should definitely be a personal experience: based on something you did or thought or heard or saw. In other words, you should be able to start it with "A few days ago . . . ." or "Yesterday . . ." or "When I was ten years old . . . ."

> The second part of the paper is the reflection. Something happened: What do you think? How do you react? Does it make anything different? Does it make you confused? (Confusion is a very good thing in this context if you are willing to admit it and investigate it.)

> These papers should be around 350 – 400 words. If it is shorter than 350 words, it will be considered "not up to standard." You will have to add to it and read it again.

> Well, that's not quite it—you will read them aloud in class. To the whole class! We will all listen, make a few notes perhaps, applaud when you finish, and then discuss.

You may cringe at this idea. You may think: I am not going to read my papers aloud to this whole class of people I don't even know. But you will. And it will be OK. It will even be something you look forward to. And you have to do it. You have to. Actually, sometimes you will read your OP in a small group rather than to the whole class.

Whether it's the whole class or a small group, everyone will support you. We will applaud. We will not (ever) comment on things that "could be corrected" about your paper. The only comments we will make will be about what you say, about your ideas. (Any comments that indicate confusion or misunderstanding should give you feedback about how your writing could be improved.)

As long as it is at least 350 words and is about you and your thinking with both a description of the event and reflection about your experience, you will get full credit for the paper. What about spelling? What about commas? What about run-ons? All that stuff. What about getting points off for errors?

None of that will happen. It won't happen because no one will see your paper. You have to have it all written out and you keep it in your file, but no one will actually look at it to read. You read it out loud in class or in your small group. That is the way the paper is presented. It is sort of like a short speech read from a prepared written text.

One last thing: We will discuss it and expect you to respond. So, you should be ready to answer questions. What did you mean when you said this or that? Can you say more about this or that? Do you feel different about this or that now?

Your Turn:

1. Before you write, read Bill's story of the first Occasional Paper in the **Personal Reflection** section. And perhaps read sample OP's in the **Resources** section at the end of the book.

2. Write your first 350 – 400-word Occasional Paper as if you were going to read it to your class.

3. Read your OP to someone else or a class you're currently teaching if possible.
What was the response? Did the class or whoever you read it to enjoy your writing? Did they understand your ideas? Did they need more information or explanation? Did they think your ideas were important? Did they laugh at the funny parts? (If there were any funny parts.)

Reflections:

1. What did you like about writing your Occasional Paper and sharing it?

_____

_____

_____

_____

_____

2. What reflections do you have about your own teaching of writing and building student interest?

_____

_____

_____

_____

_____

3. What would make you hesitate to use Occasional Papers in your instruction?

_____

_____

_____

_____

_____

4. What are your key take-away's from this chapter?

_____

_____

_____

_____

_____

Personal Reflection:

"An Afternoon at the River: The Story of an Idea" by Bill Martin

It was 1985. Besides teaching high school English to two classes of sophomores and two classes of freshmen, I had a class of 25 seniors. They were in the course known as "regular English"– a college track course for students who, for one reason or another (usually laziness), did not want to take Honors English. I treated these seniors like adults and they enjoyed that treatment. It made them feel like college students or, at least, pre-college students. I couldn't quite treat them like college freshmen given the suburban setting that included a lot of parental concern and occasional parental interference in the English curriculum, but I could get away with a lot of the bravado and bluff that emerging adults treasure. Sometimes, especially at the beginning of the period, I would try to get them to "just talk." I would open with "Does anyone have anything to say?" and sometimes (but actually not too often) someone did.

One Monday before class started, a student (I'll call him Stanford) asked me if he could read something he had written about a weekend event. I, of course, had no objections to this. After attendance, I asked him if he was ready to read. He took out a piece of notebook paper and started reading about a weekend outing with a group of friends. They went to a lake formed by one of the many dams on the Colorado River to the west of Austin. After describing some of the activities of the day: swimming, boating, building a fire on the beach, driving back to

Austin, he started reading his thoughts about this, thoughts he had as he was riding home in the back of someone else's car. He read about how this was going to be different after they all went off to college, after they became adults, had jobs, had kids, bought houses and joined PTAs. It wasn't surprising content, but it was reflective, and sincere, and authentic. And when he finished, we didn't talk about his use of detail or the sentence variety or the unity or coherence of his paper; we talked about what he had said. We talked both about the obviousness of it and also about the truth of it, the power of having said it, the importance it had for all of them. And about the different ways it affected each of them.

After we finished the discussion, I said I would give some credit to anyone who wanted to write something similar. I can't remember what "requirements" I made at this point. But other students wrote things to read. They wrote about "Misconceptions of Marching Band," "An Injury that Kept Me from Playing Football," "Being in a Group of People I Can Trust," "How Do You Know if You're in Love," "Football Dreams," "Cruelty to Animals," "What Is Passion?" "Tardy Policy," "Getting a Rush from Playing Cards," and "The Importance of Football."

The papers differed in quality, of course, also in length and reflectiveness. But they had in common a sense of authentic writing. James Britton writes that in studying composing, his team at The University of London Institute of Education at first used two categories for the degree of writer connection: perfunctory and involved. They later added "impelled," a designation for "performances in which writers made demands of themselves, so endorsing the teacher's intentions that they became virtually indistinguishable from their own" (14). In other words, the students were no longer fulfilling the requirements set by the teacher, but were fulfilling their own self-initiated purposes. The co-author of this book and I are not sure Britton and his team would agree, but we would put most of these papers in the impelled category. When students write these papers, they are writing them because they want to read them aloud. They want other students to listen to their ideas and they want to discuss those ideas after they have read the paper. There is no coercion to motivate the writing at a particular time or about a particular topic; the students have to find the motivation to write from within themselves.

Why did the students not just take me up on my offer to say something at the beginning of the period? Why write rather than just tell about what happened? I did not quite know the answer to this, and I am pretty sure the students did not have an answer either except that they were aware, as I was also aware, that there is a difference between reading aloud something you have written (therefore composed) and saying aloud something you are thinking about. The students welcomed this opportunity to "take some time" with their thoughts, organize them (at least somewhat), perform them for a listening audience, and participate in a discussion of the ideas they had introduced. That was the first Occasional Paper.

Works Cited:

Applebee, Arthur N., Anne Auten, and Fran Lehr. *Writing in the Secondary School: English and the Content Areas*. Urbana, IL: National Council of Teachers of English, 1981. Print.

Britton, James N., Tony Burgess, Nancy Martin, Alex McLeod, and Harold Rosen. *The Development of Writing Abilities (11-18)*. London: Macmillan, 1975. Print.

Dewey, John. *Experience and Education*. New York: Free, 1944. Print.

Freire, Paulo. *Pedagogy of the Oppressed*. New York: Continuum, 2000. Print.

Wells, Gordon. *Dialogic Inquiry: Towards a Socio-cultural Practice and Theory of Education*. New York: Cambridge University Press. 1999. Print.

Chapter Two

Getting Ready: Introduction to the OP Rhythm

Where are you now as a teacher of writing?

1. After reading Chapter One, how have your ideas changed about students writing about topics that make them think?

_____

_____

_____

_____

_____

2. In your teaching, are you aware of any practices you follow without being conscious of the principles that underlie them?

_____

_____

_____

_____

_____

3. Make a list of at least three trivial incidents that could be used for writing an Occasional Paper. Think about what has happened to you in the last three hours. If you're having trouble, make it the last 30 minutes?

_____

_____

_____

_____

_____

What we do:

In "Is It Time to Abandon the Idea of 'Best Practices' in the Teaching of English?" Peter Smagorinsky makes the distinction between teaching choices made in response to what are considered "best practices" and those choices made by a teacher's own personally held principled beliefs. It is true that our book proposes, and argues for, a best practice or at least a practice we have found to be a best practice *for us:*

it is an assignment with a sequence of activities that operates like a lesson plan—in fact, we call the outline of the sequence activities a recipe. But we want to be clear that we are not arguing for the recipe; we are not committed to the assignment as a stand-alone activity; what we are committed to and arguing for (in agreement with Smagorinsky) is a set of beliefs we have about students and the way students learn about writing. When we assess our teaching of writing, we do not ask ourselves "Are we following the recipe?" but rather "Are we aligning activities with our beliefs?"

To make this point Bill recounts an experience from his time as a Peace Corps volunteer teaching seventh grade boys English in Iran:

> *I was visited by my supervisor Gertrude Nye Dorry. She wrote our textbook and designed our program, and she came to observe and consult with me about my teaching. I was frustrated because my students were not making much progress and seemed interested, not in learning English, but in undermining all of my efforts to teach them. I explained to Dr. Nye Dorry all of my techniques and procedures, and she agreed with, and even praised, the design of my instruction. If I had been taking a course in teaching English as a second language and she had been my professor, I would probably have received an A for course methodology.*
>
> *However, the good methodology—the best practice—was not giving me the results I really wanted. The problem was that my attention was not on what I "really wanted" but on the teaching techniques and activities Dr. Nye Dorry had taught me. I should have instead been focusing on principles of instruction that I believed in, rather than simply focusing on approved instructional activities.*

The instructions for teaching writing using OPs are what we see as an example of how the principles we are committed to can be implemented in lesson plans and course design. We focus on OP activities because they give concrete reality to our proposal, and because it is the writing and discussing of OPs that we see as the best way to enact our beliefs. As an example, we believe that students should use writing to communicate to an audience something they really want to say. So we asked ourselves: How do we make this happen? How can this work in a real classroom? What would it look like in a planning book? And what would it look like in the grade book?

In our teaching we have found OPs can provide the lesson structure we need to sponsor the real communication we are aiming for. However, it is not the OP which we are committed to, but the communication. It is not the practice that is important but the principle.

Unfortunately, OPs can be used as part of a curriculum without students ever feeling the agency of using writing for authentic communication. Just as Bill was able to describe and justify every aspect of his teaching to the seventh-grade boys without getting what he wanted in terms of response and results, it is possible to use OPs without using them to accomplish the educational goals we think of as the motivation for using them in the first place.

Commitment to activities without a grounding in beliefs can lead us astray. But activities that seem to work can reveal foundational principles which should be recognized and followed. OPs are important to us because they are part of our way of teaching real writing as communication. They are a teaching practice we have tried, assessed, and embraced, a practice that gets us where we want to be, a practice that follows our principles. They are a concrete example of what communication in the classroom looks like.

Different ways to get there:

In this section we present several activities that will prepare students to write Occasional Papers. The obvious starting activity is to introduce an example, preferably one written by the teacher and a series of steps involved in the writing of an OP, what we call the OP recipe:

- ▶ 1. Be on the lookout for a moment that makes you stop and think.
- ▶ 2. Describe the moment.
- ▶ 3. Reflect (in writing) on its significance. (Even if you have to search for significance.)
- ▶ 4. Read your OP aloud to an audience.
- ▶ 5. Respond to audience questions about content.

This "jumping in" approach – a model and a recipe – has an appeal, but we have found that it is better to start with some introductory activities in three areas: practice in reading aloud to the class, practice in listening to other students as they read, and practice in making comments following the readings. This sequence of reading aloud, listening carefully, and talking about what has been read is the essential rhythm of OP presentations, so that is where we start. First we write simple statements. We read these aloud and discuss. Next, we use two or three sentence descriptions of an everyday incident. Our students write these, they read, and finally they discuss. Some classes are quicker to catch on to this process than others. How we begin is always a matter of reading the class we are working with at the time.

What follows is a suggested structure. We have often introduced OPs with less preparation than we present here. Classes hardly ever need more.

Part 1: Reading Statements Aloud to the Rest of the Class

We set the stage – We talk with students about what it means to write and share their writing with others. A community of Occasional-Paper writers, unlike writers on social media, both share their writing with other people face-to-face and discuss their writing with other people face-to-face. There is a physical connection as well as a textual one. To have an audience listening to the writing with the intention of discussing what is said can be both thrilling and frightening. For some students it is terrifying. For most students it takes a little getting used to. This activity will help reduce the anxiety.

We ask students to write a statement – a few sentences – about themselves that they are willing to read aloud. Usually, we ask a question rather than leaving the writing open-ended. Recently we have had students complete the stem "You might be surprised to know that…

We read our own statement first and then have students read theirs. When students are reading, we always listen to be sure that the students read word for word what is on the page – no ad-libbed additions. Students have to understand that they are reading what they have written, not talking about what they *could* have written. There is a big difference.

Here's an example of a teacher-composed statement. There's nothing "show-off-y" about it; there's no "fine writing." It's just a statement that reflects something true about the teacher.

You might be surprised to know that I have a ninety-pound black lab. She's not very well behaved because I haven't taken the trouble to train her, but she will do anything for food and she will sit quietly and let me put a treat on her nose if she is sure that when I say, "OK," she gets to eat it.

One thing we mention to students is that there should be some development – at least an additional sentence – beyond the basic statement. We usually require a total length of at least 75 words. The point is to get students used to reading aloud and to get them used to listening carefully to other people reading aloud. These statements are not OPs; they are a first step in getting ready to write and then to read OPs.

Likewise, the "discussion" is not really a discussion (even though we call it that); it is a time for a question or a clarification. Questions may range from What does the dog do that is not well-behaved? to What is your dog's name? It is just a way to get listeners used to responding to what an author has read and prepare authors for comments and questions from listeners. In order to promote and support discussion, especially at the beginning, the teacher can call on two or three students to comment or ask questions. The teacher can also keep the discussion moving with her additional comments and questions.

Part 2: Reading a Model Description of an Experience

The next step is to write a description of an experience. This is the next step because the description of an experience is the first section of an OP.

This is our lesson plan for introducing students to writing descriptions of an experience:
1. Explain to students that the first part of an OP is the description of an experience.
2. Read an example. There is an example below to give you an idea of what type of description we are talking about.
3. Tell students that they should applaud following your reading. Students usually find it a little humorous – or else just weird – that you are telling them to applaud for you, but it helps make the point that the applause is not about a positive judgment (which would mean that sometimes we might withhold our applause). The applause is just part of the procedure.

Here is a model teacher-written description of an experience:

This morning I saw a small wasp on the floor in the bathroom. It didn't fly away when I walked closer to it, so I stepped on it and killed it. I waited to see if it moved at all. It didn't, so I was pretty sure it was dead. But I still for some reason didn't want to pick it up. I got a tissue and wiped it into the folds and flushed it down the toilet.

We have students briefly write down some questions before we begin the discussion. Here are some possible questions that a student might ask about the description above:

- You said that you didn't want to pick it up. Were you afraid of it?
- You talked about it like it was not unusual. Have you seen wasps in your house before?
- You didn't say anything about trying to release it outside. Did you think about this at all?

You might notice that the example questions are in a special format. We call it the reference/ response question format. There is a "reference" to a part of the description and then the question or comment. We try very hard to get students to use this format for questions; sometimes (later in the semester) we require it. This is a learning process of successive approximations – just like the Skinner experiments with pigeons. That means that at first the students don't have to hit the target behavior; as a first approximation, any questions will do. If this type of response is new to students, it will take some getting used to, both in learning how to write down the questions and in learning how to listen so they have questions to write down. The "enforceable" aspect of discussion is that the questions should be about the content rather than the style. At this point, any questions are fine.

It is worth taking some time to explain to students how the "discussion" works. We suggest that students ask questions and make comments related to the description: things they'd like to know, things they are curious about, and situationally parallel experiences they have had. We gently steer students away from comments about the style: "I liked all the details." or "I really thought the repetition was very effective." We want students to focus on the communication: both the reading and the listening parts of communication. Communication is the core of the "discussion" event, just as it is the core of the writing and reading events; communication is where the focus should be. Once students know what it is like to communicate in this way, through writing and listening, we can introduce and practice techniques (like stylistic repetition) that make communication work better. And students will be able to tell if these techniques make (or do not make) the communication better because they will feel the impact of the technique as they read the text aloud and in the response of the audience. Praise is not necessary. Most of the time it is not even helpful.

The last thing we do at this stage is to challenge students to be on the lookout for experiences they could describe in writing. This usually sounds like fun to them, but it can also be threatening. Some students might think, "nothing ever happens to me that's worth writing about." That's why we make a point of saying that some of the best (and most interesting) descriptions are about very ordinary, very trivial events.

If students need more help thinking about topics, we provide that help with the activity that follows.

Part 3: Topics for and Writing of the "Description of an Experience"

It should go without saying, but we'll say it anyway: This activity may not be necessary; it depends on the class. Brainstorm topics for descriptions with students – experiences they have had in the last 24 hours that are "worth thinking about." Here are some examples:
- My sister said she was too tired to take me to the basketball game, so I had to walk.
- I spilled orange juice on my shirt in the cafeteria.
- A neighbor whose name I don't even know waved at me this morning like we were old friends.
- Yesterday I got an email from someone, and it made me feel really weird.
- My mother told me that my aunt is moving out of town.

Assign students to write a description of an experience (at least 150 words or half a page). The paper can be either typed or handwritten, but it should be complete, that is to say completely written out, before the class begins.

Part 4: Reading Experience Descriptions to the Rest of the Class

During this step, students read descriptions followed by applause and discussion. The meaning of applause changes from approval of the content to approval of the participation. The applause shouldn't mean "That was so great!" It should mean "We're glad you shared that."

Another consideration is whether students should go to the front of the class to read or read from their seats. On one hand, having students read from their seats eases the performance anxiety of reading to the class. It also allows a more fluid transition from reading to discussion. However, when students are reading from their seats, it may seem to leave the teacher in charge of the reading and, even more so, in charge of the discussion. If the student is at the front of the room, he or she could be told to call on people who have questions. In other words, the student could lead the discussion of his or her own paper. Another consideration is the arrangement of class furniture. If students are all facing in one direction, discussion will suffer unless the student is at the front of the room. The discussion will probably be limited to questions about the experiences, rather than an inquiry into ideas. We think that is fine. If students are enjoying this and are focused on the content, we feel we are succeeding.

This is just the first step. This is of course not yet what we have in mind as the OP assignment; what we have so far is a topic from personal experience described in some detail which is read aloud to an audience that responds to the content of the written text. To fulfill the OP assignment, we need to add a reflection about the experience, either ideas or problems, and a more developed discussion that addresses the ideas or problems that the author reflects on in relation to the experience. We have a good start toward an assignment that involves real communication, but with the addition of a reflection and deeper discussion we can say we have an assignment that asks students to write about something they really want to say and also to listen to and comment on what other students write.

The next step is the addition of the reflection which is the focus of the next chapter.

Your Turn:
After reading and thinking about "What we do," would you do the same thing or something different? What parts are problematic? What parts feel uncomfortable?

Go ahead and talk about these questions. Also, if you're ready, feel free to share what you've learned about Occasional Papers with a colleague or your students.

Reflections:

1. Review the list of topics in Part 3, and choose the one that seems most likely to lead to an idea and what is the idea?

   _____
   _____
   _____
   _____

2. Now choose the one that seems least likely to lead to an idea. Then challenge yourself to think about what larger idea can be drawn from the trivial incident.

_____

_____

_____

_____

(We anticipate possible questions, and we will include a Q and A on how to deal with those questions.)

Personal Reflection:

"Messier than Finger Painting" by Christine Gorychka

I like this passage from one of my favorite books, John Irving's *A Prayer for Owen Meany*. Narrator Johnny Wheelright elaborates on his grandmother Harriett Wheelright's opinions about reading and writing.

> *She was a passionate reader, and she thought that reading was one of the noblest efforts of all; in contrast, she found writing to be a great waste of time – a childish self-indulgence, even messier than finger painting – but she admired reading, which she believed was an unselfish activity that provided information and inspiration. She must have thought it a pity that some poor fools had to waste their lives writing in order for us to have sufficient reading material. (260)*

Throughout the book, Irving pokes fun at Mrs. Wheelright, but this passage, especially, caught my attention as a middle and high school English teacher. Like Mrs. Wheelright, so many secondary students and sometimes their teachers think writing a waste of time. For example, I was stunned while facilitating a professional development session when a small team of middle school teachers argued their case for not teaching writing during the years writing is not included in the state benchmark. Shades of Mrs. Wheelright! With a focus on reading only, it is a shame students lost a year without writing instruction and writing practice.

For many of us writing can be a "childish self-indulgence, even messier than finger painting." I enjoy indulging myself in the journey of creating text with a story in mind and words easily flowing onto the page. Or at other times, I trust my writing to take me where it wants to take me – the surprise at the end is worth it. But my writing can be messy too; the ideas fade away because I have lost interest, or the words can bump each other around and do not make any sense at all. I struggle in all the messiness but muddle through and eventually hit my stride. Then at last, I like what I have written. I read it over and over again to myself, and I cannot wait to read it aloud to someone else. I cannot wait to hear a chuckle or see a nod of agreement, perhaps any hoped-for outcomes.

 Tongue in cheek, Irving ends the passage with Mrs. Wheelright obviously missing the point, "that some poor fools had to waste their lives writing in order for us to have sufficient reading material." (260) As our students write Occasional Papers, they collect more than enough "sufficient reading material." In fact, those OPs read aloud become the vehicles for authentic communication in the classroom and the building of writing communities. Throughout our teaching careers, we have hung our hats on the principle that OPs truly teach writing as communication.

Furthermore, I believe our job as teachers is to convince our students that they are *all* communicators because *all* of them have so much to say about themselves and their lives. Anne LaMott makes the point that, "writing is about learning to pay attention and to communicate what is going on." (97) That is exactly what incorporating Occasional Papers into a language arts curriculum can do. To write their OPs, our students must pay attention, be on the lookout for "moments" or experiences to write about, and then communicate what is going on to a real audience, their classmates.

Our students certainly do not "waste their lives writing" either. Because they are encouraged to be on the lookout for experiences they can describe – anything! - they can truly indulge themselves in writing their Occasional Papers about any topics they choose. Also, they can write about topics they think their classmates would like to hear. It is true that at the beginning of a semester students may be a bit intimated by this writing assignment and reading their papers aloud to their classmates. With practice, though, and support from their teachers and peers, students settle into their comfort zones and a community of Occasional Paper writers and communicators emerge, and that is truly magical. If only Mrs. Wheelright had known.

Works Cited:

Irving, John. *A Prayer for Owen Meany.* Harper Collins, 1989.

LaMott, Anne. *Bird by Bird.* Bantam Doubleday Dell Publishing Group, 1980.

Smagorinsky, Peter. "Is It Time to Abandon the Idea if 'Best Practices' in the Teaching of English?" *English Journal,* vol.98, no. 6, 2009, pp. 15—22.

Chapter Three

First Attempt: The Real OP Procedure

Where are you now as a teacher of writing?

1. Which of these statements best captures your enthusiasm about using OPs?

    _____a) Very enthusiastic: I have tried using OPs with my classes and want to keep using them.

    _____b) Somewhat enthusiastic: I am willing to keep trying.

    _____c) Not enthusiastic: I am still not convinced using OPs is worth the time.

2. Which of these statements best captures your hesitation about using OPs?

    _____a) Not hesitant: I am willing to try using OPs after I finish this grading period.

    _____b) Somewhat hesitant: I need to know more about how Occasional Papers can fit into my curriculum.

    _____c) Very hesitant: My curriculum is jam-packed with literature and little time for writing.

What we do:

There are many, many ways to use Occasional Papers. No matter how you choose to use them, whether you choose to include them each consecutive day during a school week, or 1, 2, 3, or 4 days per week, or even use them only for a particular unit of study, it is nice to have an idea of what this actually looks like, what it feels like in the context of day-to-day classroom activities. That is what this chapter is about: to give you a vision of how OPs can fit into a school curriculum that, obviously, includes many other topics and activities. It is important to remember that OPs are different from the type of school writing where our students write when *we* decide that they should write something. OPs are written when a student decides she should write something, whether it's something she wants to argue for or whether it's something she noticed and is curious about. They are written when a student has something to say. Along with the freedom to select their topics, students need the freedom to wait to have something to say. This, of course, does not mean they can choose to never have something to say and therefore never write an OP. There are ways to put limits on the freedom to "wait until you have something to say," and also ways to put limits on when class time is available for OP reading.

Nevertheless, no matter how we have managed the scheduling of OPs, we have found that in every case we still need to be flexible in structuring the classroom agenda day by day. If we are requiring students to write one OP during a 6-week grading period (which is often the best we can do), then each class period might begin with readings of any OPs that are ready. The rest of the class period (after the reading and discussion of the OP) can be devoted to the normal class curriculum. Sometimes OPs end up dominating a class period leaving little time for other activities, and we feel okay in privileging that because of the degree of engagement involved in the discussions of those OPs. But on the other hand, many days there may be no OPs (which is always a little bit disappointing), and the entire class period will be open for other activities. We will include more suggestions for structuring class periods in other ways at the end of Chapter Six.

We have found that it is better not to start with the writing of an OP right off the bat. We usually start with some writing that will make students feel comfortable with reading aloud and used to asking questions after someone else has read. This reading aloud, peers listening carefully, and the class talking about the presented Occasional Paper is the essential rhythm of OP presentations, and it is important for students to get used to it. After that we might practice writing descriptions of an experience, then add reflections, and finally ask students to write an actual Occasional Paper on a topic of their own at a time when they want to do it. Some classes are quicker to get the feel of this than others. How to begin is always a matter of reading the class we are working with at the time.

What follows is a suggested structure. We have often introduced OPs with less preparation than we have here, hardly ever with more. Some classes catch on to this very quickly. Others do not.

✍ ✍

Different ways to get there:

Session 1: Reading Statements Aloud to the Rest of the Class

- Ask students to write a statement, a few sentences, about themselves that they are willing to read aloud. Usually, we ask a question rather than leaving the writing open-ended. A prompt that has worked well is to have students complete this sentence: "You might be surprised to know that I . . .." We encourage students to write a few sentences, but we also encourage questions and comments from the other students after each reading.

- To increase an atmosphere of support, require applause after every reading followed by the questions and comments.

- We always read our own statements first and then have students read theirs making sure that they read word for word as written: no ad-libbed additions. Students must understand that they are reading what they have written, not talking about what they could have written. There is a big difference.

Here is an example of a teacher-composed statement, the same one we used in Chapter Two. This statement says something true about the teacher.

> You might be surprised to know that I have a ninety-pound black lab. She is not very well behaved because I have not taken the trouble to train her, but she will do anything for food. She will sit quietly and let me put a treat on her nose if she is sure that when I say "OK" she gets to eat it.

Make clear to students that the point of this is to get used to reading aloud and listening to other people reading aloud. These statements are not OPs; they are a first step in getting ready to write and read OPs aloud.

The discussion is a time for some questions and clarifications. It is just a way to get students used to reading their writing aloud and responding to what someone else has read aloud.

The next step is to write about an experience since the description of an experience is the first section of an OP. We always start with a teacher-written model. This should be a fresh piece of writing.

Session 2: Reading a Model Experience Description

• Explain to students that the first part of an OP is a description of an experience.

• Read your description. Also read the following description of an experience that Bill wrote.

• Remind your students that they should applaud following your reading.

• Sometimes we have students write for one or two minutes about the model description. This can help the students really listen and usually also results in better questions and comments.

A model teacher-description of an experience:

Getting There Early

Two days ago, I was supposed to meet a friend of mine for some coffee at El Arroyo on Bee Caves Road. Since I live out by Mansfield Dam (in Apache Shores, not in Lakeway) that's a convenient place and they have good pie -- so, even though it's not my favorite place to have coffee, it is completely adequate. My description is not about the place or the time I spent talking with my friend, but about the time I spent by myself before my friend got there.

I was supposed to meet her at 4:30. But I arranged it so that I would get there at 3:45. That's not just early by a little bit but early by quite a lot. I wanted to be early "by quite a lot" because I love that time when I'm there alone in the restaurant and I can say to the waiter "I'm meeting someone, but I'm a little early" so there is no question about being able to ask for a booth. Nobody will helpfully suggest, "Would you like to have a seat at the bar?" I love sitting in a booth. I'd like to get a booth for my house. Maybe a booth and a juke box too, but

> I'm getting off the topic. What do I do while I'm there at a restaurant, early, waiting for someone I'm meeting to arrive? I write. I take along my notebook, and I write. I don't always write journal-type entries, although sometimes I do. But other times I make lists and plan things I want to do. I'm going to New Orleans for Labor Day, so I planned that: wrote down things I want to take and things I want to think about on the trip over there. I love this time: this time to sit with a cup of coffee and write. Obviously, I could do it at home anytime I want. And the coffee would be cheaper, but there is something about the surroundings and the limit of time and maybe the publicness of it that makes me very comfortable and makes me very happy.

What students might write after listening to this description:

Summary:

He talked about liking to go to restaurants early so he can write.

Questions:

1. You said that you liked being able to say to the waiter that you were waiting for someone. Why is this such a big deal for you?

2. You talked about writing plans for the trip. What other types of things do you write?

3. You said you wrote in a journal. What if you don't have your journal along with you?

You might notice that the example questions are in a special format. We call it the summary / response question format. There is a "summary" of the part of the paper that is being referred to and then the question or comment. We try very hard to get students to use this format for questions, and sometimes later in the semester require it. But as noted above, this is "successive approximation" time and not time to require hitting at the bull's eye. At this point, any questions are fine.

- After writing their summaries and questions, students should discuss "Getting There Early." They can ask questions already written down or anything they'd like to know.

- At this stage we once again challenge students to be on the look-out for experiences they could describe in writing. Sounds like fun to some students, but it can also be threatening. We make a point of saying that some of the best (and most interesting) descriptions are about very ordinary, very trivial events.

Q&A

Do students seriously have to write a summary?

The questions are more important. So if there is a choice, go with questions.
However, the summary is good training and prepares students for the summary/response format: "you said this . . . . now my question is this . . . ." We will explore the use of summary/response questions in a later chapter.

If students need more help thinking about topics, we provide that help with the activity that follows.

Session 3: Topics for the "Experience Descriptions"

- Brainstorm with students topics for descriptions--experiences they have had in the last 24 hours that are "worth thinking about." Here is an example list:

   I dropped my tray in the cafeteria and was so embarrassed.

   The power went out at my house for two hours last night; I couldn't finish my homework.

   I didn't like the movie on TV last night, and I don't know why.

   This morning my mother told me that my cousin has a new job.

- Assign students a description of an experience (at least 300 words).

- The paper can be either typed or handwritten, but it should be complete, that is to say completely written out before the class begins.

- The paper should have an interesting title, not "Description" or "My Description."

Session 4: Reading Experience Descriptions to the Rest of the Class

- During this class, have students read descriptions followed by applause and discussion.

- The discussion will probably focus on questions about the experiences. We think that is fine. If students are enjoying this, we feel we are succeeding. Students sometimes bring up parallel experiences: "A similar thing happened to me . . ." When this happens, we try to guide them into a brief discussion of what is similar in the two experiences and what is different. We do this to get ready for more probing discussions of differences within similarities. The more probing discussions, however, are probably not going to happen when every student has a paper to read. These will more likely happen when OPs start coming in one or two at a time.

Next up in this sequence is reading an actual OP. We now add some reflection to the description of the experience. Some students may have done this naturally when they wrote their descriptions. There is no way to slow some students down. This sequence may be unnecessary for some classes. But it is good to have a feeling for a step-by-step procedure even if you decide to explain OPs and then just let students dive in and give them a try.

Session 5: Reading a Teacher's Model of Experience Description + Reflection

•Start this class by reading another paper that includes a description of an experience, this time also including a reflection. We always discuss with students how this paper differs from the first one we read to them. They usually notice that there is a well-defined break between the description and the (new) second part. What should we call this second part? That is worth some discussion. Perhaps students will think of a term that makes more sense to them than "reflection."

Bill wrote this Occasional Paper (we can now call this paper an "Occasional Paper") with a reflection:

Not Something but Nothing

What Happened

When I stayed with my in-laws in northern Wisconsin in the summertime, I would sometimes go out after dark and swim in the lake alone. The water was warm and calm, and it felt wonderful to be out there in the night air, alone, in the water. But there was a strange thing that would happen when I would get far enough out so that I could no longer touch bottom: when I started just treading water and looking around. If I looked straight ahead out across the lake everything was black. There were other homes along the shore behind me, but I could see nothing ahead – not a yard light, not even a light in a window or a streetlight or anything. As I looked across the lake, it seemed like the water went on beyond my sight, on and on without an ending, without a shore to head toward. And it panicked me. Real uncontrollable panic, heart beating faster, muscles tensing. But here's the strange part: when I pulled myself around so I was facing the houses and could see lights, even though I was not closer to shore, I was immediately calm and confident. And the strangest part of all was that if I just turned again to look across the lake, I would immediately panic again. The fear was clearly irrational; I knew that I was within easy swimming distance of the shore behind me, but when I looked into the seemingly unending blackness, I couldn't help having a panic response. And perhaps the strangest part of all is that I kept doing it. I liked it. I kept turning to get that rush of panic and then turning back to recover.

What It Means

I'm not sure what to make of this. One thing it tells me is that control of fear is not the same as eliminating fear. I could control this fear by turning around, but I could not get to the point where I was not panicked when I looked into the blackness. I don't think this applies to all the fears I have; maybe it does. I always get at least what you would call nervous if not quite panicked before the start of a semester. I worry if I'm ready, if what I have planned is going to work, if I am going to make a fool of myself or pull it out and succeed. I have had this panic every semester ever since I started teaching. I think it is similar to the black water panic, but there is one difference. Even though it does go away (like the water panic) after the semester starts and predictably returns at the beginning of each new semester, unlike the water panic, I do not enjoy it.

- Teaching students what it means to reflect can be a challenge. A simple way to think about reflection is this: After describing what happened, think about how the experience affected you, what it made you think about.

  - We sometimes use this example: After I bought the expensive designer shoes, I thought about if I really needed them and returned them.

  - Then we have students to fill in this same sentence frame a few times for practice:

After I _____**, I thought about** _____.

The beauty of this sentence frame is that it is really a sentence-long OP. It has a description of an experience and a reflection about the experience. As volunteers read these, we ask them to consider whether they could (by developing the description and developing the reflection) turn this sentence into a 300-word OP. Sometimes students will do exactly that for their first OPs.

Assign students an OP (at least 300 words) that includes a description and reflection. It is really helpful to have students label the two parts. Sometimes there is not a clear distinction between the description and the reflection, but labeling each part makes it clear to readers and to the listeners. That way students will be less likely to leave out the reflection—which they sometimes do.

If you want to take this all super slow, if you want to ease the students into the big time of reading an OP aloud to the whole class, you can use reading in groups as a next step. Sometimes we go slowly like this; sometimes we skip this step. Actually, if you are going to have students writing OPs on some sort of schedule (some years we required students to have an OP every other Friday), you will probably have to do some small group readings because of time constraints. It is fairly obvious how reading in small groups works: students take turns reading their papers, there is applause, and time for comments after each one. Also, each group should complete the checklist on the next page.

Checklist to complete by one person in the group (with the help of the other group members) following each OP reading.

Author of OP

_____

Title of OP

_____

[ ] Was there a title?

[ ] Was there a description of an experience?

[ ] Was there a reflection?

[ ] Did listeners listen without distractions?

[ ] Did listeners applaud at the end?

[ ] Was there writing time?

Write two or three questions or comments that students contributed during discussion.

_____

_____

_____

_____

_____

_____

Students should hand in their OPs along with a checklist from each group. With open mic OPs, we have often not asked students to hand their papers in. This helps them focus on what the writing says rather than what the writing looks like on the page. However, there are many ways in which handing in the OPs is helpful. Handing in these initial OPs, provides a way to check for length and completion.

What will students be graded for? We have always liked to keep OP grading as simple as possible, trying as hard as possible to keep the focus on communication rather than performance. Our list of requirements for an OP to be "up to standard" are these: having the required length, having a title, having both a description and a reflection.

All the preparation is finally over. At this point, you can start the actual OP readings. This means that from this point on, students can write an OP when they come upon a topic for it. When they bring the OP to class the next day, they can read them to the class and the class will respond with applause and discussion.

Your Turn:

You are ready to give your students the OP assignment: they will need to find a topic, write the paper, and read it aloud between now and the end of the grading period. The OP should be at least 300 words and include both a description of an experience and a reflection.

Now, the next step is to just wait for students to come to class ready to read their OPs aloud.

Ask each day (each day that you have time for OPs that is) if anyone has an OP to read. There is something rather thrilling about this way to start the class when there is an OP. Suddenly the class period has broken away from the norm. The routine has been changed, and there is something special and different that is going to happen. Part of the motivation for writing an OP is that everyone loves it when someone says, "Yes, I have one."

This open mic format is the ideal way to use OPs, but it is not always possible. Luckily, there are ways to have more control over the timing of OPs: deciding when to read them, deciding when you do not have time. That is what we will discuss in another chapter.

Reflections:

1. What are your key take-away's from this chapter?

_____

_____

_____

2. How can you make OPs work in your classrooms? How interested are you in trying the open- mic format?

_____

_____

_____

Personal Reflection:
"Sample OP Starts"

The recipe for writing an Occasional Paper is this:

1. Be on the lookout for a moment that makes you stop and think.

2. Describe the moment.

3. Reflect (in writing) on its significance.

4. Read your OP aloud to an audience.

5. Respond to audience questions about content.

6. Write an author's note on your writing and the discussion.

Let's focus on what we mean by writing about an experience, looking for that moment that made you stop and think, even something that happened to you just a few minutes ago.

Each introduction below includes the beginning of a description about an experience and has the possibility of developing into an Occasional Paper.

A New State of Mind

In the beginning of the new year, I decided to make a resolution. In the past I never made resolutions or kept up with them. So, this year beginning with a new job and new classes, I decided to start working out and eating healthy. That was the main goal, but let's be honest. Losing weight wasn't the only benefit.

America's Weakness

In Kevin Weiner's article "The Testing Regime in U.S. Schools Isn't Working" he points out the main flaw of the "No Child Left Behind" program – too much testing. I always did well on the TAKS test, was in advanced classes and the school's GT program, and my teachers loved what they did. However, some of my friends didn't do as well on the tests and ended up in classes with teachers who weren't crazy about teaching and mainly showed films and handed out work sheets.

The Power of Video Games

Ever since I was a little kid, I had a game console nearby. First the Nintendo 64, and I remember spending countless hours on it and even having marks on my fingers from pressing the buttons on the controller too hard when playing a boxing game. Then I got my Ps2 in fifth grade, and that was the "best day of my life" according to my 10-year-old self.

Winter

After moving to Texas, I thought I left behind Midwestern winters – the blizzards, snow drifts, and treacherous ice. But outside my window this morning, the sky is brooding, just like me. The gray and blue clouds hold in check the cold temperature, and the live oaks normally a lush green droop in unhappiness.

Living Our Lives

According to Ralph Waldo Emerson, "Finish the day and be done with it. You have done what you could." But I have more to do. Letting all that go is tempting and lovely…and totally out of the question.

Cats Versus Dogs

My cat sits purring in my lap. Makes me think this cat really trusts me. But trusting me is different than loving me.

Give one of these "starts" a try yourself or with your class. Or maybe you found another idea for an Occasional Paper. Write and then read aloud what you've written to yourself, a pet, a friend, another teacher, or your class. If possible, listen to other read-alouds. The discussion that follows can be lively and fun!

Works Cited:

Martin, Bill. "A Writing Assignment/a Aay of Life." *English Journal,* vol. 92, no. 6, 1 July 2003 pp. 52–56, https://doi.org/10.58680/ej20031082.

Chapter Four

Inquiry-Based Discussion:
To Unpack, To Reconsider, To Discover

Where are you now as a teacher of writing?

1. Why are class discussions worth the time they take? Or, why aren't they?

_____

_____

_____

_____

2. What do your classes discuss and to what extent? Literature? Student writing?

_____

_____

_____

_____

Before we start any new practice or, for that matter, before we re-envision or revise any familiar practice, there are questions that we should ask ourselves about the practice. We need to question the relationship of the new practice to whatever we are presently doing and to assess our degree of comfort and confidence in what we are planning on doing because of adopting this new practice. We need to reaffirm that this practice is, as far as we can tell, the best practice given our objectives and circumstances within which the practice will be implemented.

The following questions and comments are certainly not exhaustive and certainly do not anticipate all the differing aspects of various situations nor do they consider differing temperaments and differing teaching styles of individual teachers, and yet these questions can be useful. They can recall other questions that should be asked or other issues that need to be faced in a change of teaching practice and, of course, it is possible that the questions cover your current uncertainties. However, these questions may not be a perfect match with those that come to your mind in contemplating a change, but we think that these questions and comments are a starting point from which you can develop your practice with confidence.

Please keep in mind, too, that some questions and responses refer to Occasional Papers or OPs, which we envision as the initiating writing activity for inquiry-based discussion. Students write these informal papers that describe something that happened to them and their reactions to it. They read their OPs aloud to their classmates and teachers and follow each reading with discussion.

Why are we promoting the idea of class discussion?

What do you do if during a discussion, a student raises her hand and asks, "Why are we doing this?"

Maybe you respond that thinking critically (which we are practicing in this discussion) will be of great value for her as she pursues her academic career, and in addition, she will have to pass this English course to graduate. Good enough answer. At least better than just saying "because this is part of the department's required curriculum." However, a better answer is (and we really believe this): Becoming better at serious discussion will make you a better thinker, and becoming a better thinker will make you a better human being.

We know that teaching students <u>about</u> thinking (as in discussion), and <u>about</u> critical thinking (as in good discussion) will help them get a better grade in their English courses and in their other courses. There is for students who are good thinkers always an advantage grade-wise, but to get a better grade does not mean to be a better person. For us to be able to say that practice in critical thinking will have such a life-altering impact, we must make the definition of critical thinking broader than coherently forming words in response to someone else's comments. In other words, we need to think of critical thinking as a form of composing, that is to say a form of making meaning. If we give critical thinking this broader meaning, then we can say that it makes our students better people because to be better at making meaning makes a person more conscious of their experience, enables them to be instructed by their experience, and makes them able to foresee the possible impact of their experience in the future. We want to broaden the definition of critical thinking to include the making of meaning.

Then, arriving at the idea that if we can think critically – having become habituated to create meaning from what we experience – we will benefit from learning to think critically in whatever life situation we find ourselves. And certainly, we and our students will benefit in any academic situation.

Why are we thinking about all of this? In the hope of making students better at discussion and making them better thinkers, and in making the world a better place.

Where do we start? Reading Aloud? *"Do I have to?"*

Let's imagine that it's Monday morning in an English class. The first order of business is the question: "Does anyone have an OP?" Let's also imagine that one student, say Christi, raises her hand and says "I have one. But do I have to read it out loud?"

An OP or Occasional Paper is an informal paper that students read aloud describing something that happened and their reaction to it (experience and reflection). Most students like to read these papers aloud. But not all of them. For many students there is hesitation and anxiety involved. And for these students reading their papers aloud is hard. For some students this is very hard. Well, how important is it?

Why not let the friend sitting next to her read it for her? Why cause the suffering?

We understand that this is difficult, but there are at least three reasons we are committed to students reading aloud what they have written.

The first reason is that we want them to have the feeling of communication with an audience – an audience who is respectful and attentive, and an audience who applauds after the reading. Hearing the applause, the reader feels, in some sense, success. It is an experience that is quite different from just writing a paper and handing it in. Even if a teacher writes an appreciative note, it is not the same. Nor is it the same as exchanging papers with someone else. Reading aloud to the whole class is an event. The class listening, applauding, and then talking with each other about the paper – it is all very different. It is also different from "talking" the OP rather than reading a manuscript.

By reading aloud to the class, a student can demonstrate membership in the class, feel a part of the class, and give evidence of trust in the class. That is the most important reason to read aloud.

The second reason for reading aloud is that the reader takes responsibility for the content in a public way. There is no way to "blow it off," to just write something to hand in with a pervading "I don't care" tone. The closest thing to blowing it off is the predictable paper about how hard it is to write an OP. However, there is a serious discussion to have about this. If the author says, "I was not really serious, I just had nothing else to write," we say, "the issue you bring up is a serious matter" and then launch into a discussion of that issue.

The third reason to read aloud is to practice a way of reviewing and revising the paper. Reading aloud allows hearing what is written and to hear it in a very amplified way when read to an audience. Hearing the words aloud and "hearing" the class listen usually allows the reader to "hear" whether or not his paper makes sense.

Reading aloud gets easier as the class gets better at listening. Of course, there is also for most students the unfamiliar but extremely satisfying feeling of having been heard, having been listened to, and connecting with these people they spend so much time with. There is a realization that reading aloud what is written is different from saying the same thing as part of a conversation. Reading writing aloud makes possible communication that would rarely happen in talk. There is power in this difference.

What makes a class discussion work?

Not only do students resist real discussion, as opposed to conversation, even when they end up for one reason or another actually having a discussion, they do not see it as valuable. What can we do about this? Of course, the easiest thing to do is to forget about discussions and stick with lectures, small group work, recitations on homework, reading, quizzes, and so forth. It is not that these activities are worthless; they can, if done well, be extremely valuable. But so can discussion be "extremely valuable." However, it takes some effort, time, and a lot of persistence to make it valuable. So the question is: Is it worth the effort, time, and persistence? Does discussion have enough benefits for students to justify its inclusion?

Gordon Wells comments that Lev Vygotsky thinks it is well worth the effort and points to the effect that public language has on inner thought (6). For students the discussion that is worth the effort is a certain kind of discussion – what Vygotsky and Wells would call "inquiry." It is worth it because it teaches us how to think. Gordon Wells goes on to say in "Dialogic Inquiry in Education: Building on the Legacy of

Vygotsky" that thinking (according to Vygotsky) is first done in public language (out loud) and then it is internalized as thought (6).

There are two ways we can guide a discussion, two ways it can improve thinking. One way it improves thinking is by giving us access to other perspectives, to the workings of other minds molded by differing and individually unique life experiences and ways of thinking--ways of thinking that are different from our own. In this sense it broadens the application and corrects for ego-centric narrowness. The second way it improves thinking is by giving students an opportunity to "be heard," to be listened to and responded to. In other words, students are given a chance to be taken seriously as thinkers for their intellectual skill.

How can all students – those who like to talk and those who do not – become engaged in a discussion?

Some people, some students, are gifted at discussion, at seeing concepts and articulating ideas, and other students are not. Does this mean that discussion is great for some, but not engaging for others? Yes and no. Engagement is certainly crucial. Without engagement there will be no benefit. Those that are already "good at it" will be engaged because they know how to do it. For the rest, engagement must come from other sources. One source is experience. Although they may not be skilled in discussion, they have had different life experiences from everyone else in the class, and depending on the topic this different life experience can be uniquely valuable to the richness of the discussion.

In his article "All Writing Is Autobiography," Don Murray claims that because all writing grows out of life experience, the life experience is always relevant: the contributions of a unique intellect, of a radically personal way of knowing life, will always be relevant in discussion (67). The person who brings this to the discussion can rightfully feel like an intellectual, and as a contributor to the project has a clearer understanding whatever topic is at hand. A student who writes an Occasional Paper that includes a description and reflection about a personal experience is a contributor, with the opportunity to become fully engaged in a discussion.

What is the teacher's role during a class discussion?

This is where the teacher is important. The teacher needs to be sure that the discussion does not devolve into vacuous abstraction and keep it rooted in life experience. This means some manipulation of topic choice and perhaps a manipulation of the topic once it is chosen. In addressing a topic, we should ask:

"What does this mean to our lives?"

"What is it like in our (*our own*) experience?"

"How will recognizing it change the way we respond to our experiences?"

If we ask for, listen to, and apply the addition of each person's life experience, students will have a reason to engage in discussion and through discussion add to their repertoire of "cognitive instruments" for thinking about life. The desired (and entirely possible) outcome will be that students will be able to use these cognitive instruments in their writing and their thinking.

The key to engaged discussion is to focus on student experiences – not just describing these experiences but analyzing them, comparing them, drawing from them guidance in dealing with future experiences, and through them enriching our understanding, understanding the place of these other experiences in our lives and in the lives of others, to know our own lives better by seeing them in relation to others' lives.

Why can we not expect dialogic inquiry from the get-go?

Our students are not thirsty for philosophy; our classrooms are not Athenian agoras. We are facing a population of smart-phone obsessed, hormone driven, distraction prone, grade motivated auditors. They are not disposed to, or inclined to, inquiry. They may have no sympathy for civil discourse and no aspiration to be calmly curious and intellectually modest, so we cannot expect what Gordon Wells might call true inquiries (9) from the get-go, not at least without some pre-selling of this type of classroom talk.

That they are not naturally or culturally predisposed to inquiry as a stance from which to explore reality may be true, but it is also true that the reality that is their life now and the concerns which they bring with them to class and take with them when class is over, their hopes, their annoyances, their connections, and their feelings of isolation or inclusion are all topics which they will (perhaps timidly) be interested in examining. Using class time for this examination might seem almost a subversion of school curriculum; we usually have a few students who leave the classroom at the end of a semester saying, "we may not have learned much about English, but we learned about life." So, we should be willing to let them think they are getting away with something as we guide them and in fact join with them in dialogic inquiry. Dialogic inquiry can be a way of learning about life. But we should not start with an explanation of dialogic inquiry or even with rules for our discussion. The first step toward inquiry is to generate discussion.

How do we generate discussion and get to valuable inquiry?

The first thing we want students to do to progress toward the goal of true inquiry is to talk. To talk to each other. To talk in an orderly way one at a time and to listen to what others say. In other words, to talk with civility. We want our students to want to do this, to see it as valuable, and to see it as enjoyable.

We will start by asking them to talk about their real-life concerns, to tell their classmates what they are thinking about and to find out what their classmates are thinking about the same topics. We have found that the better they know each other and the more they can respond to each other as human beings with a shared interest rather than as competitors, the more easily they will adapt to civil interchange. Insofar as we have a method for achieving this after the "ice-breaking" talk, it consists of writing brief papers called Occasional Papers about their concerns, reading these papers out loud to the class, and listening to and participating in discussions of the topics of these papers by classmates.

What counts as a "good" discussion?

The primary objective of discussion is to start with saying something, to hear that voice in the classroom. The content of the comments or at least the quality of the comments is not crucial. They should be relevant, and they should follow from what precedes, but they should not be judged and certainly not evaluated. That gives us some behavior to start with, behavior that we hope to refine and mold into true inquiry. We might follow this initial talk with a sequence of invitations: "Feel free to ask questions" for instance. We model this with our own questions and reinforce this invitation by inviting "dumb" questions, devil's advocate questions, obvious questions. We want students to free themselves of the obligation to "perform" and feel good about asking questions prefaced with "I'm almost embarrassed to ask this, but I will ask it anyway." In fact, we often offer the students a list of question starters:

"You may have said this already but...."

"I'm probably the only one who doesn't get this but...."

"If I were explaining this to someone else, I would have trouble explaining...."

Especially we want to encourage the use of a request for amplification:

"You said (such and such) and so my question about that is this...."

We are tempted to think that when we want to up the ante in class discussion that we should take on more complex, more abstract, more philosophical topics. But we think the better path is to make the thinking and the questioning more complex, more philosophical, and more abstract; and keep the topics as concrete, immediate, and homegrown as possible. The higher-level thinking comes from the way we discuss rather than what we discuss.

We look for understanding, but that starts with information first:

"When did this happen?"

"Has this happened before or since?"

"Can you describe anything more about a person's state of mind?"

"Does it happen or could it happen in other situations?"

This is newspaper stuff: Who? When? Where? How? And maybe Why? It is gathering information. A part of this understanding level of discussion might be similar experiences that other students have had. What was common to both experiences? What was different? There are more discussion starters in the Resources section at the back of this book.

A discussion such as this would count as a good discussion. Students listened to what the author had to say, and they asked pertinent questions and described similar experiences. No need to pursue things further at this point. But after many discussions at this level, we may want to push for more inquiry, more probing questions, more hard thinking about a topic. As we pursue this, we want to be careful not to push the author too hard; we don't want to have him or her feel attacked or make him or her want to say "You're making too big a deal of this. I'm sorry I brought it up." But instead, we want to push the topic further, so we are not really talking anymore about the author's experience, but we are working together to explore the described experience and how we react to such experiences:

"What do we do with these experiences?"

"Can we talk about them with other people?"

"Do other people understand what we are talking about?"

"Do we remember them?"

"Do we value them?"

"How can we make sure we remember them and value them?"

"How does it feel to share them?"

This is the sort of self-questioning of experience we are hoping for and working toward.

What is the place of civility?

While our initial goal is to get our students to talk, our second goal is to get them to be quiet, to get them to listen. The discussion should be at the same time civil, critical, and consequential. That is to say, there should be listening as well as speaking and rationality rather than ranting. (It should be civil.) And there should be honest challenge and requests for clarification. (It should be critical.) And there should be expansion or elaboration, in other words change of understanding. (It should be consequential.)

Consensus is intentionally excluded from the list of desired outcomes. Consensus is not necessary. However, change of some sort for all the participants *is* necessary. The change could simply be a sharpening of a student's stance, some clarification for his or her own commitment. In other words, it does not need to be a reversal of thinking, only a change in thinking. Changing our mind in some way means the discussion was (for you) not a waste of time. In fact, being the gadfly, the naysayer, the one who challenges what seems to be self-evident is a position which should be highly valued and highly honored. In other words, it is good to be, as Sheridan Blau would say in *The Literature Workshop*, "as stupid as you really are." You may hesitate to say "I don't get it, can someone explain it to me?" An automatic response might be "What don't you get, it's so obvious!" when it is only obvious to the common way of thinking. The fact is that nobody else gets it either, or at least that you are not alone. There is also no privileging or valorizing of "winning" the discussion.

The most important thing is to eschew consensus because it stops discussion and thinking. If a class gets good at this, there should always be a challenger, a devil's advocate, ready to question what seems to be a slippery slide toward cordial but premature agreement. Understanding is deepened in the reading as well as discussion by consideration of other ways of looking at an idea. There should always be:

"What if…."

"How does this help?"

"Is there something being lost in looking at it this way?"

"Is this loss necessary?"

"Does it apply to all human situations?"

And so forth. There are always questions to ask.

What about lapses of attention? What about non-participation?

Good listening is part of participation, and there is no need for everyone to speak in order to call something a good discussion. But for the whole thing to be carried by only four or five people is a sign that we need to make an adjustment. So what to do? Your students can take time to write, take time to consult with one or two peers, take time to report back and reframe the idea under consideration.

We think there is great power, probably also great wisdom, in letting nonparticipants choose to remove themselves from active participation without punishment. (This does not mean letting them go to sleep or leave the room.) We are content to have them simply listen. but only if their non-participation does not become disruptive.

What about the other extreme? What about a student who talks too much, who dominates the discussion? This is a violation of civility but should probably not be addressed by punitive grading. It brings up the issue of turn-taking and who gets to determine who speaks. It should also be appreciated that the way this is handled in a large group, possibly the teacher redirecting the discussion, could solve the problem. When the teacher is available to only one small group at a time and the group can't resolve the problem on its own, the small groups can ask the teacher to make a guest appearance and temporarily take charge of the discussion. This problem is often ameliorated for large groups and small groups by the self-evaluation that students complete at the end of the discussion period.

How do we step forward in a discussion and then step back?

In classroom discussions, as in any cognitive project, perspective is of crucial importance. To see something from one perspective is usually not enough to enable us to know, or to understand, what we see. Not only do we need to see something in three dimensions, but we also need to see it from different angles and through the multiple lenses of temporal change.

As we discuss something in class, it is appropriate and potentially very helpful to step closer to the topic and then to step back from the topic. The discussion itself is of course helpful because, since there are many students involved in the discussion, it is inevitable that many points of view will be offered and that each of the students involved will see the topic differently. But all these slightly different perspectives can be enriched by stepping forward and stepping back.

Take as an example the statement by one student in her Occasional Paper that she loves her dog. What can we do to interrogate this seemingly innocent and non-controversial statement? In conversation we would be considered socially tone deaf to subject this to inquiry, but in an inquiry-based discussion social conventions such as this must not be abandoned. We need to question this statement, not to discount it, falsify it, or reject it (although these are ultimately all possible reactions), but to unpack it, to reconsider it, to discover what it *could* mean and what it *does* mean. "I love my dog" she writes, and supposedly she goes on about the dog and the love in some detail, but let us suppose we are left with the simple declaration of love for the dog. How do we explore its meaning? First we can step closer:

"What sort of dog?"

"How old is the dog?"

"How long has it been your dog?"

"In what sense is it your dog?"

"Do you buy its food?"

"Do you take responsibility for its health?"

"Do you groom it, exercise it, or train it?"

All of this is factual information that helps us know what we are talking about.

Then after stepping forward, we step back. That is, expand the context. There are several possible ways to do this, but all of them are potential contexts for the question "What difference does it make?" We step back to see the big picture, to be able to answer the question about what difference it makes:

"Does this love have a value for the student?"

"Is having a dog a good thing (in the big picture)?"

"Should every child have a dog?"

"Are there other pets which have the same value?"

"What is the best kind of pet?"

"What is the best kind of love of a pet?"

"Is being a pet good for a dog?"

"Why do we have pets?"

"What different places do pets have in our family structure?"

"Should we refer to them as 'companion animals' instead of 'pets'?"

By stepping closer we make clear what we are talking about. We define the topic at least for the purpose of our discussion. By stepping back we contextualize, we see the topic in relation to the individual lives of the people involved and in relation to the human condition, in relation to the infinite complexity of human concerns. In other words, we learn how to recognize the need for information, the evaluation of information, the relevance of information in a particular context, and the effect that valid and relevant information can have on our thinking.

What makes a discussion successful?

The key to engaged discussion is to focus on student experiences – not just describing these experiences but analyzing them, comparing them, drawing from them guidance in dealing with future experiences, and through them enriching our understanding, understanding the place of these other experiences in our lives and in the lives of others, to know our own lives better by seeing them in relation to others' lives.

Our discussion may likely be and will hopefully be about ideas, but we will do well to also bring them into contact with real lived experiences. How do these ideas affect our day-to-day lives? What difference does our attitude toward these ideas make? If we are discussing procrastination (a common topic in high school discussions) "What difference does it make?" is a question worth asking, and "What difference has it made?" is also crucial to consider. From experiences with procrastination, we can develop our own individual attitudes towards it. We can think about the causes, the remedies, and the consequences. We can also discuss the common judgment about it and the reason for that judgment. We should also consider when and how procrastination can be a benefit. Certainly there are some good things to say about procrastination. This all will be a richer, more reliable, and more interesting discussion than a predictable study-skills-based collection of common attitudes that students have become familiar with and perhaps internalized from cautionary adult advice, for example (good students make a to-do list and stick with that regimen).

When does a discussion become dialogic inquiry?

Experience of others that we know and a stance of inquiry about the meaning of our different experiences can not only be the foundation of good discussion but also can help us achieve a more ambitious goal: intellectual inquiry. Students will learn how to talk reasonably, question each other civilly, and through the modeling of this interested and engaged talk, learn how to think about abstract ideas by relating them, not to other abstractions or to aphorisms, but to their own life experiences. This is inductively constructed theory constructed by working from evidence to principles: this is good thinking, and it is the basis of, and is modeled by, good discussion.

In inquiry-based discussion, there are no opposing sides in competition with each other. Everyone is on the same side working toward the common goal of enriched understanding. This does not mean there is no questioning, no doubting, no skepticism. In fact, there is more rather than less of this type of pursuit because it is a pursuit of understanding. It is in the service of digging beyond the surface of what passes for conversation and revealing the complexity and, in most cases, the indeterminacy of knowledge and what passes for understanding. We are all working toward a deeper understanding. Even though we will never reach a final understanding of a capital-letter truth.

How do we avoid slipping into conversation?

Some of our impulses, our conversational habits, need to be repressed or revised if we are to engage in real inquiry. The success of inquiry is always earned by the whole group engaged in the inquiry, not by individuals, and what the group needs to do to achieve success is to keep the conversation going in a thoughtful way. And to enrich understanding.

This means continuing an examination of a topic without lazily sliding off onto a different topic: to extend inquiry vertically rather than horizontally, going from the literal to abstract. We are not used to doing this. Conversation builds horizontally, one thing leads to another, everyone can add to the chain of contributions. Inquiry works differently. It is not conversational, and, in a sense, it is antisocial in the erasure of ego. It is also the very pinnacle of community building interchange. Understanding is a group project.

In conversation, comments can be linked associatively. ("That reminds me of something that happened to me…") But in inquiry (working vertically) the linkage should tend toward clarification and logical connection.

To clarify we ask:

    "What do you mean?"

    "Can you give an example?"

    "Are you saying 'this' is different from 'that'?"

To connect we look to the implications and applications:

"What does this mean for the larger question of X?"

"How does this make a difference in the way we think about X?"

"Could it be that Y…?"

Did anything change, did anyone's thinking change because of the discussion? This question is the right one to ask. Something should change. Otherwise, it is simply sharing rather than an interrogation or examination or adjusting of ideas. Somehow, we should come away from a discussion thinking differently.

We are trying to understand each other, not trying to convince each other, and by understanding each other, to deepen our own understanding. We might ask where this all stops. Of course, it *does not* stop, so when do we stop the discussion? We cannot look for agreement, for consensus, as a way to end the talk because that may not happen. So how do we end? We think it best to end talk with an invitation to continue it. And the best way to continue is by returning to the topic through some writing. All of this may seem to be a buzz kill or a snooze trigger. It should not be.

What should be the basis of evaluation for discussion?

It cannot be making comments or how many comments are made. But rather it should be evaluated based on the students listening to comments. Listening sounds easy. But as we all know, it is not easy. It involves focus and requires comprehension.

The first impulse is to quiz students, but in many cases, this will measure hearing rather than listening. And it is of course true that hearing is essential. But hearing is not the same as listening; repeatability is different from understanding. To evaluate listening we need to deal with meanings rather than words.

Listening is easy when the content of what is being said is familiar and is easiest when the context is shared. It is hard, however, when the context is shared but the responses to the context are different. If both the speaker and listener have new puppies to train, listening to a discussion about puppy training is easy, but if the speaker likes the new puppies and the training challenge and the listener wants to get rid of the new puppies and escape the hassle of training, then listening may be difficult.

So we can evaluate by asking students for analogies, examples, and questions, but although we can evaluate these parallel constructions as successful or unsuccessful, this is not the point. The point is to teach students to listen and then to test their own listening. Perhaps we can ask small groups or partners to come up with analogies, examples, and questions through collaborative construction based on group inquiry.

Listening, then, is best nurtured and supported by topic choice and interpersonal relations. The more we know about the topic and the speaker, the easier it will be for us to listen. We include more about listening and evaluating discussion in other chapters.

Finally, we end this chapter hoping we have addressed some of your questions about discussion and given you the tools to build Occasional Paper classrooms with confidence and joy. Along with writing OPs and reading them aloud, students need to talk to each other and listen to each other as a community of writers. We also know that class discussions about student writing take time and patience, and most importantly waiting for those moments when talk evolves into inquiry. For your students to realize that they want to talk more, they have not reached a consensus, that's okay. With a new understanding of each other, they deepen their own understanding of new ideas and want to continue the inquiry. That is almost magical …you hate to see the class end. But an Occasional Paper a couple of days later can continue the discussion.

What are two ideas about discussion you are taking away from this chapter? Or, maybe you have more questions?

1. _____
   _____
   _____
   _____

2. _____
   _____
   _____
   _____

Works Cited:

Blau, Sheridan. *The Literature Workshop: Teaching Texts and Their Readers*. Portsmouth, NJ: Heinemann. 2003.

Murray, Donald. "All Writing Is Autobiography." *College Composition and Communication,* vol. 42, no. 1, Feb. 1991, pp. 66-74.

Wells, Gordon. "Dialogic Inquiry in Education: Building on the Legacy of Vygotsky." *Ontario Institute for Studies, University of Ontario,* 1997, pp 1-31.

Chapter Five

Skills Without Drills

Where are you now as a teacher of writing?

1. What is your responsibility as a writing teacher to offer your students choice in usage and mechanics? When, if ever, do you require manuscript correctness?

_____

_____

_____

_____

2. Whether you require it in student writing or not, what is your attitude toward teaching the correct nominative or objective case? Let's take one example, what is your tolerance for students using "just between you and I" rather than the correct "just between you and me"? Are there other conversational "errors" that bother you in student writing?

_____

_____

_____

_____

What we do:

When students think about becoming better writers (if they ever think about becoming better writers), they might think about the mechanics of punctuation, the process of proofreading, or the importance of vivid word choice. This does not necessarily do any harm, but it often does little good. It does not inspire enthusiasm or eagerness for correcting mechanical errors.

We have thought about this problem in the following way: learning to write is like learning to dance. Of course, there are many obvious differences between learning to dance and learning to write, but there are also some possibly helpful similarities. So, we are going to develop this idea of writing and dancing. Maybe we should narrow the idea to learning to improve as a writer is like learning to improve as a dancer. We learn to dance, at least in part, by watching other people dance and by wanting to dance like other people. So, it is the combination of observation and imitation.

Someone who is not interested in becoming a dancer or in becoming a better dancer will not learn much from watching other people dance. Possibly it will be entertaining, maybe even delightful, but it will not be instructive. A dancer, however, will not watch other dancers in the same way as someone who is not a dancer. A dancer will watch other dancers for ideas about dance, for ways to improve, and for moves to add and adopt to his or her own dancing. This dancwer will, in other words, observe other dancers, not as an observer but as a dancer. In a similar way we can teach or at least encourage our students to read like a writer. Reading like a writer is to read other people's writing for ideas about your own writing. Reading like a writer is to be sensitive to what in your reading is making an impression on you, what seems powerful or persuasive, what is memorable or surprising. Then you may at first awkwardly, but eventually successfully do the same thing in your own writing. For this to actually change a writer's writing, the writer has to be writing a great deal: producing a great deal of writing and a great deal of low stakes writing. This is exactly what we have in an Occasional Paper classroom: students who are writing a lot and in a way that will support experimentation. Students may flounder instead of flourish or give their writing organization that is not successful or possibly nonexistent, but they will not be penalized for these attempts. They will be writing in an environment which supports experimentation.

Different ways to get there:

Reading As a Writer:

We can teach reading as a writer by having a class or small groups look for and comment on moves to imitate student written texts or professionally written pieces. But this only teaches the method. The real power of this way of learning to improve student writing is when a particular move in a text that a student is reading gets his attention and he decides to imitate the move in his own writing – just like the dance move he would like to imitate and add to his own dance moves. The power is in self-selecting what the object of imitation will be and applying it to the writer's writing in a self-selected way.

Stylistic Choices

Students should learn to frame what they admire and wish to imitate, that is to isolate the example by putting a frame around it so to speak. Then to name it, which is useful for recall and for access later, and finally to make it their own in their own writing. In other words: name it, frame it, and claim it. That is the formal structure. But the important thing is to be able to shift your reading from comprehension of the written text to admiring and borrowing the form of the written text. There is very little that you need to learn about writing that you cannot learn from other writers if you learn to read as a writer. All you need is a text that is in the same genre as your own writing and an attitude of experimentation.

When you are reading as a writer, you are of necessity looking for stylistic choices that you can access when there is an occasion to use them. You then add them to the toolbox for writing that you maintain and remember that they are there. It is possible to set out on a writing project or a revision project with the intention of making use of a certain stylistic move. But it is worth remembering that simply making a particular move will not automatically make your writing better. It is for this reason that we can say that reading as a writer makes you potentially a better writer but does not automatically make your writing better. Reading as a writer does not answer the predictable complaint that using OPs neglects skills in the use of punctuation, vocabulary, or sentence structure. Nor does reading as a writer really address the organizational requirements of written presentation. The benefits are increased, however, when students share their experiments in the use of professional writing as a model. It is also an opportunity for group work where students take a professional text and frame a move to imitate and then perhaps see if each person in the group can find a place to use the imitated move in revision of their own writing. Who knows whether their writing will be more powerful or more persuasive, and if it isn't, just noticing the possibility of change and then making a choice is certainly worth something.

Models of Good Language

There are many ways of teaching skills without drills, but two things are (almost) always required. There must be models – not necessarily sentences or text presented as models but language that is used well, that you notice either in what you read or what you hear being read by others. There must be models of good language use that show care about the content and show care about the audience. And there must be practice in using the stylistic choices in the right places. The second thing is this means doing a lot of writing and it also means doing a lot of reading. It means seeing yourself as a writer.

Presentation

Although Occasional Papers foreground the content rather than the style or correctness of the writing, good writers do at some point have to concern themselves with presentation. And it is because this is part of our obligation as language arts teachers that at some point content is shelved for a moment, and rules, drills, writing handbooks, and corrected papers enter the picture. It is at this point also that for many students the enthusiasm for writing is diminished or even destroyed.

If presentation is addressed by reading as a writer, although it may seem less efficient in covering all the bases, it is more efficient in covering only the bases that the writer sees a need to cover and therefore will internalize. Reading as a writer puts the student in a position of agency. She chooses the writing moves she admires or finds useful. She then seeks occasions to make use of these moves in her own writing. Since for most students the subjects of their OPs are those they care about, and the audience for most students consists of people they care about, there is a shift from careless writing to more careful writing. Thoughts and motivation to improve and the motivation to retain the means of improvement is strengthened.

Reading as writers, motivated students focus on one or two "moves" to incorporate in their writing, including manuscript correctness. An Occasional Paper classroom offers all kinds of opportunities for students to read as writers – to compare their writing to that of professionals or other students: to name, frame, and claim an example to imitate. Making stylistic choices, looking for models of good language, and focusing on presentation and manuscript correctness are what students who read as a writers do. In fact, students can improve their writing simply by reading a lot and writing a lot.

Your Turn:

From your reading, choose a model of style or language that you want to imitate in the next Occasional Paper you write. In other words: name it, frame it, and claim it. Write your OP including the imitation. Read your paper aloud to yourself a few times to hear your imitation of a particular move. If you're brave enough, read your OP to your class and afterward share your story of choosing a particular model of language to imitate. Be sure to explain what you had been reading that inspired you to choose the model to imitate.

If you feel comfortable with the **Your Turn** assignment, try it with your students. Arrange them in small groups and find short texts for them to read and then discuss stylistic moves and models of language they want to imitate. Next, have your students write and present their short paragraphs of imitation. If some of your students want to take the imitation to the next level, they can write Occasional Papers that include imitation of a stylistic choice or model of language from something they have been reading. Again, who knows whether their writing will be more powerful or more persuasive, but making the attempt is certainly worth something. Finally, the more students read and the more they write, the more likely it will be that they will become better writers and will think of themselves as writers.

In the **Resources** section, you can find examples of professional authors that your students can imitate as they read as writers.

Reflections:

1. How comfortable are you with the idea of your students and you reading as writers? Check all that apply and if you want, add comments and/or questions.

_____a) I think direct teaching of writing skills and drilling students on those skills is very important and should not be replaced. I'm not comfortable with asking myself and my students to read as writers. To me, reading and writing are separate entities.

_____

_____

_____b) I had never thought about teaching writing skills by asking my students to read as writers. But I have also directly taught writing skills and wondered how effective my teaching really was.

_____

_____

_____c) I really like the ideas presented in this chapter and will try the Your Turn assignment myself and then with my students. I'm still not sure about taking the time to include OPs in my daily lesson plans so that my students can experiment in their writing. Required writing assignments take top precedence.

_____

_____

_____ d) I plan to make the time for including Occasional Papers in my curriculum so that my students can read as writers and experiment with their writing. As we write, we also will be reading literature required in the curriculum, and my students will choose books to read independently. With minor adjustments, students should be able to move through required writing assignments more efficiently.

_____

_____

Personal Reflection:

> ### "Seeing Myself as a Writer" by Brianna Look Hogan
>
> *Brianna was a student in Christine's AP and Creative Writing classes, and she wrote Occasional Papers in both. Thirteen years later, she reflects about the impact listening to her classmates' Occasional Papers had on her writing.*
>
> I think my first impressions of the process were maybe intimidation. The thought of writing so frequently – something that wasn't an assigned research-type project and reading out loud, I'm sure caused some trepidation at first. But I do remember feeling comfortable once we did get to reading out loud, and certainly listening to everyone else's stories and feedback. It felt bonding.
>
> I do recall thinking I no longer wanted to write using cliches or wanted my writing to sound young or childish. I think that's when I started to edit myself more, tried to write with a more consistent voice. I also remember feeling very influenced by other students' writing – the way they were able to capture feelings/emotions/descriptions that I may have not thought of before.
>
> I feel like writing more often and about a variety of topics made my writing better. I know I moved away from over flowery language. In my current role, which I wouldn't necessarily consider "writing heavy," it still comes into play. I find myself editing all the time, trying to get points across in a more direct way, and removing superfluous language. I think your class was the first time I felt my writing was growing up and sounding more grown up.

Chapter Six

Two Weeks of Occasional Papers in a Twelfth-Grade Classroom

Where are you now as a teacher of writing?

1. What has been your experience (if any) fitting Occasional Papers into your lesson plans?

_____

_____

_____

_____

_____

_____

2. What has been your biggest challenge or what do you foresee as your biggest challenge? From colleagues? From the administration? From your students? Or what has stopped you in using Occasional Papers?

_____

_____

_____

_____

_____

_____

What We Do:

Bill kept his lesson plans and notes during a two-week segment of one twelfth-grade English class. Here are some of his comments, questions, and details of the day-to-day Occasional Paper presentations in this class.

Q&A

How do you grade OPs? In the description of your reminders to the class, you said how in the first two weeks they are 100s. What is this about?

In order to encourage students to write their OPs before the end of the grading period, we use a graduated grading scale that reduces the optimal grade every two weeks. During the first two weeks the highest grade is 100. During the next two weeks it is 90, and so forth.

Deductions are also possible for an OP that is too short or an OP that doesn't have a reflection. These are 10 point deductions.

Look at the Grading chapter for more possibilities and ideas.

Week 1, Monday and Tuesday: The students were already comfortable with writing OPs, reading them aloud in small groups, and discussing them. But during the first couple of days of the open mic agenda, no one had OPs to read aloud to the entire class. This is always disappointing, but it is also not unusual. If students can wait until they have something to say to write their papers, then we have to wait for them to do that.

Week 1, Wednesday: I was tired of waiting. I reminded students of the OP requirement (one written, read, and discussed by the end of the grading period). Some of them were still stuck on the idea that the topic had to be something remarkable, something really momentous. We did some topic brainstorming of things that had happened since the students got out of bed that morning. For instance, they couldn't decide what shirt to wear, or they were out of their favorite cereal and had to eat toast, or their mother surprised them with the idea of going out to dinner that night.

Week 1, Thursday: An OP! It's from Tory, "What's Bugging Me." Her friends are bragging about colleges they are applying to, and her boss is hiring people she doesn't like. Not much reflection. In any case, it started things off. And since it was a "complaining" OP, it is going to inspire some more. Students love to write about other people's shortcomings.

It's worth saying something about discussion at this point. After the applause is over, what happens? Who starts? At the beginning of the year, I usually say "Does anyone have a question?" And if no one is ready to ask something, I always have a question to ask. It is an uncomfortable and unpleasant feeling to have just read an OP that you think is good and then have complete silence from the people you read it to. It is important to avoid this, even if it means that you, as the teacher, always have the first comment. However, later in the year I often don't say anything, challenging students to fill this gap. I just sit there and wait along with the students. Usually someone will step up to the plate and ask something. If not, of course, I don't leave the author of the OP dangling there for too long. I'll ask a question if necessary.

This OP did not take too long, so we still had time to work on the regular curriculum, the writing of arguments. We talked about using occasions in day-to-day life not only to find topics for Occasional Papers but also for arguments.

Q&A

How do you choose between homework time and OP time?

I don't want to punish students with less time to do homework in order to read OPs. (Actually, I seldom give homework time.) Students like OPs, but I don't want to force them to "pay for" the OPs with more homework to do outside of class.

This is important because I want the feeling (which is usually what I get) of everyone hoping there will be OPs. I also want students to want to talk about them. I don't want students to be thinking, "I don't want to talk any more because I need to get the homework done."

The crucial question is whether you as a teacher think OPs are important or not. If they are important, they should be treated as if they are important.

This may mean some juggling of time in class for homework. OPs do require you to be somewhat flexible.

Week 1, Friday: Next day, no OPs, so we used the class time for silent reading and at the end of the period, some students talked about the books they were reading. I reminded the students that next week would be the second week of OPs; therefore, the final week of 100s for OPs. We reviewed some hints about finding topics:

> Someone **says something** that makes you think.
> *The clerk at the 7-11 calls you "Honey."*

> You **see something** that makes you think.
> *A boy throws down an empty drink can, and someone else picks it up and tosses it in the recycle bin.*

> You **read something** that makes you think.
> *The newspaper has an article about eating crackers from ground cricket flour.*

> You **remember something** that makes you think.
> *The dark clouds on the horizon make you think of when you lived in Denver and a snowstorm was on its way.*

Week 2, Monday: Four OPs! I wondered whether we should we read them all or put some off for tomorrow. The primary classwork was beginning group work on the awareness of audience. This involved students individually reading some material in the textbook and an example essay. I decided to make the individual reading assignment homework and use the class time for reading the OPs. A guide I do not always follow but always think about is that individual reading and writing can be done outside of class, but reading of OPs and discussion cannot. Of course, neither can group work, but we will be able do that tomorrow. (FYI, I don't assign a lot of long homework assignments every day.) This is another challenge to your ability to be flexible.

- The first OP was "Silence." It was about "what counts as silence." The idea was that we hardly ever, probably never, experience absolute silence. Some discussion of ambient noise and elevator music and sounds of nature.

- Second OP: "Guilt Kills." It was about two kinds of guilt: culturally imposed guilt (not your fault) and self-imposed guilt. I didn't make a note of the "occasion," so I don't know how this came up, but it was a good discussion. (For most of these OPs, I did not make a note of the "occasion" since the discussion centered on the reflection. The notes I make are to prepare myself for the discussion.)

- Third OP: "Government Should Ban Alcohol." This came up because of a news article about drunk driving. The discussion headed toward how legislation would work. I deflected this (because we are not lawyers and can't know what is really legislatively reasonable) into talk about who wins and who loses: the general good vs. individual freedom.

- Fourth OP: "Normal." What is normal to some is unbearable to others. Taking good health for granted. Taking privileges for granted. Is "happiness" normal?

This took most of the class period. I reminded my students about homework (the reading from the textbook) before the period ended.

Week 2, Tuesday: Next day there was one OP. The rest of the time they needed for group work. I told them that next week we wouldn't have OPs on Monday or Tuesday because they would be doing presentations about topics from the regular curriculum.

- OP: "To Be a Parent." About sacrificing for your kids. Why would anyone want to have kids? What is "good enough" parenting?

Week 2, Wednesday: The next day after the class period with the "Parent" OP, there is a "follow-up" OP: "Why I Want to Be a Parent." I loved this so much. I love it when the students start using OPs as a way not just to communicate but to converse. There is after all much more to say about most of these topics than what can be said during a single discussion.

- OP: "Why I Want to Be a Parent." About seeing what it means to her parents. Wanting the same troubles and joys she sees her parents experiencing.

Week 2, Thursday: After my elation about the follow-up OP, the next day brought me back to earth. There was an OP, but it was just a description with no reflection. It felt a little like an OP written because the student had to get one written rather than an OP that the student really wanted to read to the class. This happens. It's not the end of the world.

- OP: "Stalkers and Fans." About a phone call of appreciation (after a concert at which the student performed) from someone she does not want to hear from. Difficulty of setting boundaries when the annoying person is being so flattering. There was no reflection. The OP was just a description of the incident.

Because there was no reflection, there was a grade reduction of 10 points. The discussion was, however, very good.

Week 2, Friday: Next day there were two OPs. Reminder that there will be no OPs on Monday and Tuesday.

- o OP: "Write Anything." About writer's block. This is not my favorite OP topic to listen to or discuss. (It seems someone always ends up writing about this – a sort of meta-procedural and predictable move.) And there are usually a couple of these during the grading period: papers about the "experience" of not being able to write a paper. At this point it is too early to get harsh about this. And the discussion can try to explore what can be said about this in contrast to what is usually said about this: trying to bust through the cliché. In any case, I steel myself for the inevitable trope about having nothing to say so you have to just say something about not being able to say anything. There is just a description of the problem so reduced credit on this. Not much discussion; I didn't push this beyond the cliché as I should have. Maybe it's my fault there was no discussion. I was just so unenthusiastic.

- o OP: "Life." Another predictable OP on "stopping to smell the roses." However, this one does have an incident and a reflection. The fact that the reflection is not very deep does not prevent it from starting a good discussion and getting full credit. In the discussion, we try to push deeper, beyond the cliché. I was able to pull it off this time and use the "teachable moment." We considered: What is usually said about this? What else is there to say? What other ways are there to think about this? What does it take to move your life in this direction (to be more aware)?

The notes on this two-week period may not make everything clear, but they do demonstrate that doing OPs in this way takes a sense of adventure and a whole lot of flexibility, not to mention a good system for remembering where each class "got to" in the continuing lessons of the standard curriculum.

For students to remember where their classes "got to", they keep a class notebook that is graded every grading period. For each OP they write the author's name, the title of the OP, and their ideas for questions. Also in their notebooks they make an entry every day including the homework, the vocabulary, reading notes, writing drafts, and other daily notes.

Keep in mind the following:

☞ You can have OP-free days designated when needed (as for the presentations.)

☞ Some OPs deserve special consideration to be read immediately. For instance, the OP that was in response to an OP on the previous day.

☞ There will be more OPs (surprise, surprise) at the end of the period for 100s, or other plateau points. This is inevitable but is preferable to having all the OPs come in during the last week of the grading period.

☞ Worth considering: When the classroom is partially "owned" by the students, they will be more willing to buy into the part the teacher "owns" for traditional lessons. Therefore, the time "sacrificed" for OPs may actually buy you more time of focused attention.

☞ Finally, it seems very important to us that there is always time for discussion. Reading the OP without discussion is not worthless, but it misses an incredibly rich teaching moment.

> ***Discussions answer questions such as these:***
>
> *What more is there to say?*
>
> *What are the different ways to think about this?*
>
> *What makes a good critical comment about this topic?*
>
> *What was not clear in the OP? (This is not addressed directly but through a request for clarification: "When you said X, I wasn't sure what you meant.")*
>
> *What was memorable and interesting in the OP? (Also not addressed directly. But it is obvious from the discussion and even just from the way students listen, what we found interesting and what is going to stick in our memories to be – perhaps – brought up later.)*

The questions above are good starts for class discussions. Also, we have included three "Discussion Guides" in the Resources section at the end of the book.

Different ways to get there:

If you're not crazy about the open mic format, or you tried it and it didn't work for you, we have several different ways to incorporate Occasional Papers into your curriculum:

1. Reading OPs in small groups:
   We almost always use small groups at some point, particularly at the beginning of a semester when some students hesitate reading their OPs aloud to an entire class.

2. Scheduled day for OPs:

>An obvious solution is the scheduled "OP Day." Just allow OP readings on Fridays or every other Friday or whatever day you choose. It's not ideal (in our minds), but it will work.

3. Signing up:

>You can also require students to "sign up" to read OPs so that you know in advance how much time is going to be needed each day.

4. Limit on number of OPs to be read during a single class period:

>Maybe you will find that one OP a day is workable. So you allow that, but no more than one. (Or maybe two.)

5. OPs read at the end of the class:

>This solution is far from the being the best option because it inevitably curtails the discussion. It doesn't work for us (and we have both tried it). But – who knows – maybe it will work for you.

6. DIY:

>You can, especially after you experiment with OPs a little, probably think of other solutions to the OP unpredictability problem.

7. Diving in:

>Then there is the radical idea of just diving in and making it work. If you choose to do this, there is the other side of the unpredictability coin: the pleasure of it. As we already hinted, there is just something wonderful about being able to start each class period with the question "Does anyone have an OP to read today?"

>Students look around to see if anyone is going to read. Almost always it is exciting to everyone if there is going to be an OP (or two or three), and almost always it is disappointing if there is no one ready to read. This becomes a motivation to write: everyone wants you to write, everyone wants there is be an OP. You are writing not for a captive audience but an eager, receptive, and grateful audience.

Your Turn:

If you haven't already, choose one way to incorporate OPs in one of your classes. Ask a partner to do the same. Take and keep your notes like Bill did for a couple of weeks. Then share your notes with each other and discuss what worked and what did not in each of your classes.

Reflections:

1. What is your comfort level with the open mic format?

A: No way! Not knowing how many OPs we would begin a class with and keeping up with the grading was too much for me to handle. Plus, I found discussion difficult. I probably talked too much and didn't have confidence that my students would discuss each other's writing. I need more structure, and all five of my classes must cover the same material each day. However, I will try putting students in small groups to share OPs I assigned.

B: I tried the open mic format in one of my five classes for two weeks. It was interesting to see how many OPs were read each class period. I found it easy to keep up with adjusting class time for the regular curriculum and the grading made sense. Discussion made me uncomfortable. I didn't insist to my students that it was their responsibility to become interested in what their classmates were writing and to ask questions and make comments. Oops! No wonder. I forgot to ask my students to take notes as papers were read.

C: I tried the open mic system in 3 of my 5 classes and found I could manage the time element and grading. Handing discussion over to my students was tricky. However, I found if I began the discussion with a good question or comment and one that was particularly inviting and easy for students to jump on, my students took over the discussion.

D: I love the open mic format and use it in all my classes.

Chapter Seven

The Real Deal: Experience, Reflection, and Revision

Where are you now as a teacher of writing?

1. What is it about Occasional Papers that challenges the way you teach writing?

_____
_____
_____
_____

2. What benefits do you anticipate and what reservations do you have about reading your own OPs aloud to your students?

_____
_____
_____
_____

3. What reactions have your students had to reading their OPs aloud to one another?

_____
_____
_____
_____

What we do:

Although you may by now have some idea about what an Occasional Paper (OP) is, how it looks, and how it sounds, you may still have some questions and maybe some reservations about how and whether you would use Occasional Papers with your own classes. We hope to address some of those questions and reservations by looking closely at what goes into the writing of OPs in a normal classroom setting.

We will explain this in a series of steps. These steps, however, involve only the discovery of a topic and the writing of the OP; they do not include anything about discussion which we feel is as important and, in some ways, more important than the writing. Chapter 4 – "Inquiry-Based Discussion: To Unpack, To Reconsider, To Discover" includes many strategies a teacher can use in an Occasional Paper classroom to initiate discussions, redirect discussions, and elevate discussions to a more intellectual frame. There are also three Discussion Guides that include discussion starters and other tips in the Resources section.

Even though the OP recipe is simple, and the introductory activities can be helpful, students are at first going to have an incomplete picture of this process. We always tell our students to relax and trust that eventually everything will be clear. We don't know whether you are comfortable with that way of running a class, but whether you admit it or not, that is what is going to happen: the students and the teacher will eventually discover through engaging in the activity how the activity works for them.

Different ways to get there:

Step One: The Topic

Once you start writing OPs, you have to be on the lookout for a topic all the time. The topic will come as a result of something that happens to you or that you observe; it will be something that may make you stop and think: "There's something interesting about this, but I'm not sure what it is." We all have these moments, but when we do, we usually only get as far as thinking "this is interesting." Much of the time we don't even get that far. We will, given the way most of us live our lives, seldom go beyond this initial thought to really exploring what there is in this moment to explore. OPs get us beyond this momentary curiosity to the stage of making meaning – exploring, developing, and questioning the experience. They allow us and even force us to be conscious of our life experiences. In this sense OPs can be and have been life changing.

But you must avoid the trap of the extraordinary topic. If you were asked right now to come up with a topic that is "worth writing about," you might respond by reviewing in your mind the interesting experiences you've had lately, things that are in some sense "highlights" or "events": a vacation trip, a visit from an old friend, going to a concert or play or party – experiences worth posting on Facebook or documenting with selfies. This is a trap.

This is NOT how you should start looking for an OP topic. At least it is not the start we encourage students to make. We tell them that they need to simply watch out for something as they go through their day: not something exciting or remarkable, but something that makes them (or could make them) think. That is the key. Anything that makes you consider, reflect, wonder even for a moment is the starting point for an OP. OPs require, and therefore develop, a habit of mind: a habit of openness and awareness.

Now the examination of these moments doesn't always pay off. You can't predict what will yield an interesting reflection before you start writing. We tell students to bring to mind something they could write about. It is probably the case that the sorts of things we are referring to are not things that happened last month or even last week. The moments we are looking for may make a person think but do not seem significant enough to make a person follow that thinking for very long. You are aware of them for a minute or two and then they are gone. Therefore, rather than reviewing events from the previous week or month, it is better to look back over a single day or even the last two hours. You are more likely to find these "diamonds in the rough" in the very recent past.

The claim we are making in promoting such topics for OPs is that if you do think about these "insignificant" things, these rough diamonds and develop your thinking in writing, you will be rewarded with insight. It might not always happen, but it will happen more often than you might expect.

So, what is an example of an "OP experience"? Suppose someone chose the following experience concerning her dog:

> *The dog came in with a toy in his mouth and looked at me. I told him "Not right now." He went into the other room and lay down.*

Do you suppose that if somebody had read to you the description above you would be eager to think, wonder, consider, or explore the incident? Probably not. But the important point for a writer of an OP is not "is this experience going to be interesting to a reader?" It is, instead, did this experience make me think? Did it puzzle me when I experienced it? Maybe it was only for a second, but that is what you are going to write about; you are going to take this mundane experience and give it some meaning. The "moment" described above is just a starting point.

Where could a writer go from this starting point? Perhaps the writer would wonder in writing what made the dog suddenly want to play and then so easily give up. Perhaps she wondered what went through the dog's mind once she refused to play with him. As she wrote about this, she might begin to think about how much of what she assumed was going through the dog's head was actually just what would go through her head. In other words, how much did she – how much do we – start to think of dogs as furry humans and forget that they are a different species?

Whether that line of thought would be or would not be interesting to you as a reader doesn't matter. The thing that matters is that it is interesting to you as an author. We are confident, after many years of listening to and writing OPs, that by pursuing it, the author can come up with some ideas that really are worth writing about. Ideas that are interesting. Ideas that will make this a good OP.

What are some other examples of OP moments?

> *I saw an empty Budweiser can along the street as I was walking through my neighborhood. What were my thoughts? Litter. How attitudes toward littering have changed. What would it take for someone to feel OK about throwing an empty can into the street in front of someone's house?*

Not a front-page story, but it is material for an OP. Here are some other possible OP moments:

- ☐ A friend recently decided to eat a vegan diet.

- ☐ There were ashes in the middle of the street from a small fire evidently from last night.

- ☐ When I woke up, I thought it was Monday and then realized it was Sunday.

We don't want to give the impression that all OPs have to be about what students would call "random" topics. If someone dies, it is certainly worth writing about the reaction you might have. If something wonderful happens: a new job, a new love, a new baby, it would clearly be a worthwhile topic for an OP. On the other hand, if the national news about jobs is pessimistic, an OP about your reaction would make sense. There is nothing in the "requirements" for an up-to-standard OP about the topic being sufficiently trivial. It is just that this is the mindset we want students to have: whatever the topic is, there is the possibility of making meaning.

The topics we discourage are topics that are not directly related to our day-to-day experience, topics about which we have too little first-hand information to be truly reflective. Familiar school writing topics such as capital punishment, addiction, climate change, or the Civil War are probably not good topics for OPs. On the other hand, an afternoon visit to the Gettysburg Battlefield might be a perfect topic, as would a reaction to hearing Jane Goodall comment on climate change.

Once a writer gets the idea of writing about moments in day-to-day experience, there is no such thing as having nothing to write about. If it seems like there is nothing to write about, the writer just needs to think harder about, and look more closely at, what is happening in his or her life. OPs help us to open our eyes and open our ears and open our minds. As OP writers, we need to relax the filters that favor the extraordinary over the quotidian.

We help students find topics by having them write down five "moments" that they remember from the past 24 hours. If nothing comes, rather than expanding the time under consideration, we tell them to reduce it: remember some moments from the last two hours instead of the last twenty-four.

If students have trouble thinking of five, we tell them to loosen their minds, to be a little playful. Look on an unpromising topic as a challenge. Nicholson Baker wrote a whole book about what happens to a man on his lunch break. Look what Isaac Newton (at least according to legend) made of an apple falling on his head. Proust wrote hundreds of pages about a single dinner party, and an OP can be up-to-standard with only 300 words. Just 300 words! This should be easy.

Just for fun, have students choose something that seems to hold no promise and see if they can make it work. Take the challenge: it may seem that there is nothing to say, but you can try to find something. You can try to make something.

Step Two: The Description of an Experience

After identifying a topic, the next step is a written description. We give the following instructions and observations to students before they write:

> **Describe the incident vividly and dramatically. Use whatever specific details and dialogue you can remember. This is both for the benefit of listeners and also for your benefit: the more clearly you remember the "facts" of the situation, the more material you will have to work with in exploring its meaning or importance.**

We remind students that the "meaning" of the moment – the value of thinking about the moment – will usually not be obvious until they start writing about it and discussing it. It's hard to say for sure that something is not worth writing about before you write. More likely you could say that you are just not interested in it right at that moment. Maybe at that moment it's you that is not interesting. And that would be fine. It's best, however, to try a little harder before you give up. It's okay to have a question without a clear answer.

Here's an example of a written description that could start an OP.

> *I was sitting at my desk typing on the computer when my dog came in. I had just taken him for a walk before I started working, but he now brought me a tug-of-war rope, holding it up to me, and looking at me expectantly. When I said, "Brandy, not now" he turned around and lay down in the hallway.*

Notice that there is nothing "reflective" about this step. This first section of the paper is intended to be purely descriptive. It can be a completely chronological account of the simple occurrence, but it should include as much detail as possible. We, of course, don't ever want to make the rules more important than the writing, so if a student writes reflectively in this first part we don't see that as a problem. However, the important point is that writing the description not only nails down the experience but also gives the writer time as she is writing to let the experience feed her reflection. You don't have to have the meaning worked out before you start writing. You can discover the meaning.

It's important for students to describe as accurately as they can. It may be that not all the detail is important and also possible that all the detail won't make it into the public draft of the OP, but if it's written down, it is there to use, and if it isn't written down (being that it is not about anything "significant" – at least not yet), it will probably be forgotten.

Should you try to do some "fine writing"? Something eloquent and impressive? This is tricky. Certainly, there's no harm in letting yourself go to that "fine writing" place if it seems natural to do that, but you don't want to get stuck trying to think of a beautiful first sentence or a startling analogy. Better to get it down with some awkwardness and some clunkiness. Just try to get it all down; eloquence can come later if that is what you want.

How long should it be? What should you try to include? What should you try to leave out? Look at this more developed example of the dog moment:

> *My dog, Brandy, came into the study where I was working on plans for next se-mester. I had just taken him for a walk before I started working, but he now had a rope in his mouth that he likes to play tug-of-war with. He held it up to me with an expectant look in his eyes. I said to him, "Not now." He turned and walked into the hallway and lay down dropping the rope in front of him and laying his chin on his paws.*

Not bad. We could, of course, develop it more. There is always something to add. We could add more about the circumstances: description of Brandy, time of day, the mood, urgency of getting plans done, how much attention Brandy had had during the day so far. Here's a third try:

> *My black lab, Brandy, came into the study where I was working on plans for next semester; I was trying to get at least the general outline finished before the weekend. I had just taken him for a walk before I started working, but now Brandy had the rope that he likes to play tug-of-war with in his mouth. He held it up to me with an expectant look in his eyes. I didn't want to be interrupted, and I said to him, "Not now." He turned and walked into the hallway and lay down dropping the rope in front of him and laying his chin on his paws, still looking up at me.*

That's better, but at the same time the previous attempt is also perfectly OK. If we take another shot at it, we can probably develop it some more. Writers are never going to reach a point where there is no possibility of further development. For now, the "still looking up at me" attempt is fine. There's more time for revision before this is made public.

What if students can't reach the 300-word goal for describing an experience? Well, Rome wasn't built in a day. This process isn't magic. It may take some time. But we believe that if students give it another chance and perhaps another chance beyond that, they will find the writing comes more easily and is both satisfying and valuable.

Step Three: The Reflection

By the time a writer finishes the description of the incident, she might or might not have some ideas about a meaning. We say "a" meaning because any incident, any moment, could be given many different meanings. An author of an OP has to consider the incident and answer the question **"What would I like to talk about with someone after describing this incident?"** or the question **"What ideas are suggested by this moment?"** We encourage students to just venture in, to just start writing and not to be afraid to change their mind or reject a line of thought that seemed promising at first. We tell them to imagine that they are trying to provide an account of "a mind at work." We tell them if you find yourself resorting to a cliché (Dogs are truly our "best friends"), don't reject it, instead admit it, question it, re-state it, and dig deeper into it. Clichés often stop reflection by seeming to settle things: "Absolutely! Isn't that the truth! Those dogs are so loyal." Admit in writing that you have a cliché and deal with it. "I am finding myself wanting to say that dogs are people's best friends, but I know that is just a cliché. What does it mean? Would a human friend do what my dog did? Why is it that my dog is so 'understanding' without, in fact, understanding anything about why I won't play with him? Am I that understanding (without understanding)?"

Reflection is a matter of asking questions and then asking questions about the answers to those questions. There is no formula for reflective thought. But perhaps you can teach it – or at least encourage it – through example and, during discussion, through initiating inquiry that pushes thinking deeper.

Here is a model of a description plus a reflection:

Description:

My black lab, Brandy, came into the study where I was working on plans for next semester; I was trying to get at least the general outline done before the weekend. I had just taken him for a walk before I started working; now he had the rope in his mouth that he likes to play tug of war with. He held it up to me with an expectant look in his eyes. I didn't want to be interrupted and I said to him, "Not now." He turned and walked into the hallway and lay down dropping the rope in front of him and laying his chin on his paws, still looking at me.

Reflection:

My first thought about this moment is that I'm glad I have a dog that "gives in so easily." Other dogs might not "get it" and keep pushing the toy at me. I also think about how I felt somewhat guilty even though I had just taken him for a walk before I started working. But the thought that is just sketching itself in the back of my mind now is whether this dog behavior is something to look at as a possible and desirable human behavior. If I wanted to talk to someone (a friend), and she said to me "Not right now," and she said it with no explanation, how would I feel? When parents say this to children "Not now, sweetie," how do the children feel? Is it a good lesson to learn? Should I, as a parent, want my child to hear such a refusal and "give in" without any question? Of course, we want our children and our friends to have a sense of being important in the world. However, we don't want that for dogs. I obviously can't explain to Brandy why I don't want to play right now, but I can explain to a friend or a child, and I should. It seems obvious that we shouldn't treat our friends or children like animals, but we, in fact, often do. A dog is unquestioning because it is not in control of circumstances. Human beings should be questioning, and we should want them to question, even if we sometimes wish they would be more like dogs.

That's a lot of reflection. It just started rolling out. The reflection does not have to be that long. But if you as a writer are on a roll, don't stop yourself.

After we read this model, we have students silently reread their descriptions and start a new paragraph with the heading "Reflection" or "What I think of this."

Some advice for students who are not quite ready to write: Stay loose. Don't necessarily try to be wise and philosophical. Just try to consider deeply. If you are familiar with freewriting, you know the trick about rewriting the last couple of words you just wrote when you can't think of what comes next. In writing a reflection a similar trick is to "talk to yourself" as you write. You might write "I feel like I'm heading into a dead end here. I'm going to change course a little." Or you might write "Is this interesting at all? Well, I don't care. I'll write it out first and then get selective about it." You might choose to leave this bit of self-conferencing out when you read your OP to the class, but if you leave it in, that's OK too.

Step Four: Revision

We don't kid ourselves about our student writers. Many, many of them write their OPs and read them without revision. We don't require revision of standard OPs, and don't check for it (we will get to for-mally presented OPs in Chapter 8 – "Stress-Free Grading"). But what we tell students, and what seems to make sense to them, is that they should read their OPs out loud to themselves before reading them out loud to the class. Nevertheless, there are students who do not revise their OPs. We always suggest revi-sion to students, and we always revise our own OPs before reading them to the class.

What we tell our students:

> **Read your OP out loud to yourself. Revise it for both clarity and rhythm. Listen to how it sounds as you read. It should have the sound of a thoughtful human voice. It should have the sound of your voice as a writer. Don't try to "show off." And remember you are revising it for an audience of listeners. At this point there is no consideration of a "publication" in print. You are not going to type this up and distribute it. You are revising your paper by reading it aloud to yourself so you can read it aloud to an audience.**

After having done the hard work of composing a first draft, it is true that to make yourself read out loud to revise is really hard. It's hard enough to get yourself to reread at all, even silently. You are not, after all, proofreading for spelling errors or punctuation – except where spelling or punctuation errors are go-ing to make it difficult for you to read your OP to the class without stumbling. Reading out loud is easi-est if you have someone to read your OP to. It's best if you can actually read it out loud rather than read-ing it "out loud" inside your head. It's best if you treat it as a dress rehearsal for an in-front-of-the-class performance. This rehearsal will improve your reading and also improve the OP that is on the page. There is very little doubt that it is worth the effort. However, convincing yourself that it "is" worth the effort is often difficult.

Two more points about revision:

1. Students should not feel they must revise to eliminate the false starts or other indications of their "thinking process." Very often, if they are explained in what they write, these "errors" will actually help their readers understand. Even though we used the term "performance" in the discussion above, we want to stress that the reading of this Occasional Paper should be an act of communication, not an act of performance. The false starts, the revisions of the main

point, the concessions and reservations can often communicate a writer's thinking much better than a more pared-down, more refined text.

2. Encourage students to read their OP aloud to someone willing to ask questions and enter into a discussion about the content of the paper. This may lead to revision before they read to the class. On the other hand, students should not think that they have to anticipate and therefore preempt all possible questioning. After all at least one of the points is to initiate discussion.

There you have it – an Occasional Paper that includes a description of an experience and a reflection about that experience. It began with an exploration of possible topics and ended with a little revision: The Real Deal

Your Turn:

One aspect of our suggestions for using OPs in class that may bother you and perhaps cause you to dismiss the whole idea is that students read OPs when they have been "moved" to write them, giving you no way to plan how much time to allow for OPs during any one class period. With the open mic format, how can you stay on track with other demands of the curriculum when every day may have a significant "interruption" from two or three OPs? And how do you keep track of several class sections of the same curriculum being at different places, never "in sync." What do you do? You may think this is not worth the trouble.

But hold on, and we repeat there are several ways to make the assignment of OPs more manageable. Here are some ideas we have mentioned in Chapter 6 – "Two Weeks of Occasional Papers in a Twelfth Grade Classroom." Why don't you choose two or three that might work for you.

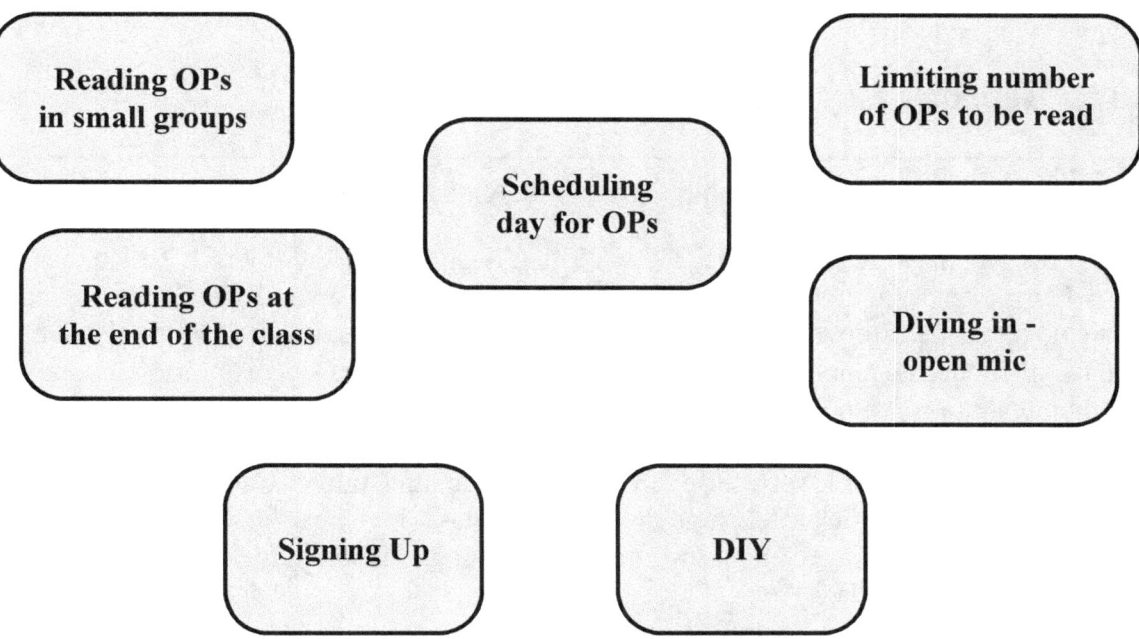

Reflections:

1. Why would students be impressed that you're a bit embarrassed about reading a "not perfect yet" OP aloud to them?

_____

_____

_____

_____

_____

2. What bugs in the OP assignment do you still have to iron out?

_____

_____

_____

_____

_____

Personal Reflection:

"Saving a Teaching Career" by Kim Hensley Owens

Many people who have read Bill's article "A Writing Assignment / A Way of Life." in the *English Journal* or heard a presentation about Occasional Papers have adopted and adapted the assignment successfully and have been enthusiastic in their response. Several OP advocates have published accounts of using these papers in their classes. We want to share one compelling testimony from Kim Hensley Owens, a professor at the University of Rhode Island, who added OPs to her teacher development courses. She writes in personal correspondence that "it's been rather lovely, fitting this personal, fleeting, non-critiqued oral narrative into college classes that don't often have that kind of thing. I love hearing them; I love sharing them; I've learned so much about my students that I never would have known otherwise." She goes on to tell this story.

I have the future K-12 teachers I teach each fall read your article, too. It's a K-12 teacher in my native Arizona I wanted to tell you about, though. She was a favorite student back when I taught high school there in the late 90s, and since she graduated college, she's flirted with various graduate programs and teaching locations over the years, finally settling in to teach high school for the last few. Last year, though, she was ready to call it quits, and we ended up chatting on the phone about that. Her school's curriculum is quite scripted, and as a former YAW-Per (the young adult version of NWP) she wanted to do lots of writing, particularly personal writing, with her students, but she couldn't fit it in with all the other things the school and the testing climate required. She wasn't feeling like she was getting any of the good stuff from teaching, only the hard/bad stuff.

I told her about your article and suggested she try Occasional Papers as a way of getting a bit more personally connected with her students, and as a way of getting more writing in without taking up too much time and without increasing her grading burden. She started doing OPs the next quarter, and she loves them, and recently told me I "saved her teaching career." Since all I did was suggest she try something you suggested, really YOU saved her teaching career. So thank you for that, and for all the stories my students have shared and will continue to share. OPs really are a way of life.

Works Cited:

Martin, Bill. "A Writing Assignment/a Way of Life." *English Journal,* vol. 92, no. 6, 1 July 2003, pp. 52–56, https://doi.org/10.58680/ej20031082.

Chapter Eight

Stress-Free Grading

Where are you now as a teacher of writing?

1. Which areas of your teaching writing affect your students the most?

    ____ a) planning writing lessons

    ____ b) delivering writing lessons

    ____ c) interacting with students about their writing

    ____ d) grading student writing

    ____ e) evaluating student writing at the end of each grading period

2. Which statement below best describes your grading of student writing?

    ____ a) I hate grading my students' writing, especially writing comments that I know they won't read

    ____ b) Once I get started grading my students' writing, I can finish in a reasonable amount of time. Starting is difficult.

    ____ c) I usually stagger assigning essays to my classes. That way I have a smaller stack to grade at one time, don't feel overwhelmed, and get papers finished in a timely fashion.

    ____ d) I enjoy grading essays and work efficiently during my lunch breaks and planning periods. Also, I use a rubric to lessen writing comments.

    ____ e) I use an online grading system that I really like. I can briefly scan individual assignments and post grades.

What we do:

John Dewey writes "there is a big difference between having something to say and having to say something." Arthur Applebee makes a similar point when he says that the best writing lessons are motivated by "a need to communicate . . . something the author wants to say," and that secondary school writing programs could be improved if more of this "natural" writing were included. He adds that the inclusion of this type of writing is the program adjustment that is "the most difficult to implement." The idea common to the observations by Dewey and Applebee is that writing motivated by a sincere desire to "*say something*" is the basis for the best type of writing instruction. We call such writing "real writing" and characterize it as writing that is driven by a desire to say something rather than a need to fulfill requirements. It is making use of writing skills to communicate rather than simply to demonstrate skills that could be used "at some later date." This distinction between communication and demonstration has been a guiding focus for us in the development of our secondary writing curriculum and in our development of Occasional Papers.

Our students enjoy writing Occasional Papers, reading them aloud, and discussing them in the classroom. As they read and discuss, we have seen the confidence of these students increase as well as their trust: trust of their classmates, of their teachers, and of themselves. We have found that we can provide the benefits of Occasional Papers in our curriculum without being burdened by additional and time-consuming marking and grading of papers. But, for us, the enjoyment, the positive attitudes, and the flexibility are not the main reasons to use OPs. The main reason we use OPs is because they provide students with a chance to actually use writing to communicate rather than simply to demonstrate competence. Students get a chance to use writing to have an impact on an audience, rather than writing simply to demonstrate what they could do if they were writing in response to a real communication need in a real communication situation. We have seen how students who know what it feels like to write in this way, enjoy writing, look forward to writing, and come to think of writing as an opportunity, rather than an obligation.

However, we know that students also respond to grades. Many students like earning good grades and will respond positively to a grading structure. In the next section are several ideas on how to incorporate simple and flexible grading systems for Occasional Papers into an established curriculum. What can look like a "completion grade" though, is more than that. There are basic requirements for the paper to be up to standard. A "100" designates whether or not the OP has met the basic criteria. Yet teachers will not have to mark and grade stacks of papers in the traditional sense.

Different destinations:

Grading Occasional Papers in an Open Mic Classroom

We typically begin the class by asking, "Does anyone have an OP to read?" We never know how many hands will go up, hopefully at least one and not more than three. If there are more than three volunteers, we ask one or two of those students to delay reading their OPs until the next day so we can move to other activities scheduled that period.

We require that everyone pay attention to an OP when it is read aloud. This means no open books, no shuffling of papers, no heads down on desks. Applause follows each OP: the applause is not about the quality of the OP, but the support of a writing community. Also, after each OP there is a short writing time, usually no more than three minutes, sometimes as short as one. Students should have their writing equipment ready so that they will not have to dig for materials. Basically, students summarize what the point of the OP seems to be and then write comments and/or questions about the content of the writing. It is not a time to evaluate the OP or criticize the author's writing style. Here is a handout we use with our classes. Sometimes we use a daily journal to record the same information.

Title of OP and Writer	What is the writer's main point?	What questions do you have for the writer?	What comments do you have for the writer?
OP #1			
OP #2			
OP #3			

Discussion begins with level one questions, those that stick closely to the facts of and feelings about the incident described. Eventually the discussion should explore the meaning and importance of the incident and when possible, extend into philosophical principles which connect to the meaning of the incident.

During a six-week grading period, we use the sliding scale (below) giving students credit for the required two Occasional Papers. Each OP should be at least 300 - 350 words long. During the first two weeks, the highest grade is a 100. Then during weeks 3 and 4 the highest grade is a 90, and during weeks 5 and 6 the highest grade is an 80. Obviously, we encourage students to write and read aloud their OPs early in the six weeks; otherwise, rooms full of teenage procrastinators will wait until just before the grading period ends to read their Occasional Papers. Plus, we will have to rush through discussion to get all OPs read and discussed.

Grading Occasional Papers for 6 weeks

Week One	1st OP - 100	2nd OP - 100
Week Two	1st OP - 90	2nd OP - 100
Week Three	1st OP - 80	2nd OP - 90
Week Four	1st OP - 80	2nd OP - 90
Week Five	1st OP - 80	2nd OP - 80
Week Six	1st OP - 70	2nd OP - 80

Keeping in mind that Occasional Papers are to be 300-350 words long, a student can lose 10 or 20 points when the paper is not long enough, or when the OP does not include a reflection, or when it does not include both the description of an experience and reflection about that experience. The student's grade with a minus 20 depends on where he/she is on the sliding scale, and no grade is ever lower than a 70. Traditionally Occasional Papers are not handed in. This helps students focus on what the writing says rather than what the writing looks like on the page. However, there are advantages to having the paper copy submitted even if it is not going to be graded as a written draft. Having OPs turned in guarantees that papers are fully written out (not partially ad-libbed) and can provide a check on the length and completion. Additionally, handing in papers can give full credit to students who were ready to read their papers, but time would not allow.

At times with large classes and curriculum constraints, we abandon the open mic format, and our students share their Occasional Papers in small groups. If that is the case, students should hand in their OPs. Also, each group should complete and hand in a checklist, like the one below, for each OP that is read.

Checklist to complete by one person in the group (with the help of the other group members) following each OP reading.

Author of OP

_____

Title of OP

_____

      [ ] Was there a title?
      [ ] Was there a description of an experience?
      [ ] Was there a reflection?
      [ ] Did listeners listen without distractions?
      [ ] Did listeners applaud at the end?
      [ ] Was there writing time?

Write two or three questions or comments that students contributed during discussion.

_____

_____

_____

_____

_____

_____

We like to keep OP grading as simple as possible, trying as hard as possible to keep the focus on communication rather than performance. It should not take long to look through a stack of Occasional Papers handed in that day. To be recorded as a 100-completion grade, an OP must be "up to standard" by meeting the following requirements: the required length, a title, both a description and a reflection.

<u>Grading Occasional Papers for a Formal Reading</u>

By the end of the third week, most students find writing Occasional Papers easy and even enjoyable, and then feedback from their peers even more enjoyable. Students seem to love seeing the smiling faces of their peers and hearing them laugh (when they're supposed to) during the reading of an OP. Also, there is nothing better than hearing applause after a reading, followed by questions and comments from the rest of the class. Sometimes another student will write an OP in response to an OP already read aloud. Close to the end of the grading period if you choose, you can have students participate in a Formal Reading. Preparation begins with each student choosing one Occasional Paper to revise. That could be anywhere from increasing the paper in length by elaborating on what's already there, to developing a new idea or two to add, or to developing a totally new OP using the topic of an OP already read in class. Whatever the selected option, we arrange for our students to read their Occasional Papers in a more formal setting than the classroom, usually a small auditorium with a podium, so that students stand in front of their audience to read.

In revising an Occasional Paper for the Formal Reading, we encourage our students to try this revision strategy:

❖ Read the OP out loud to yourself.

❖ Revise it for both clarity and rhythm.

❖ Listen to how it sounds as you read. It should have the sound of a thoughtful, human voice. It should have the sound of your voice as a writer.

❖ Don't try to "show off." And remember you are revising it for an audience of listeners, your classmates.

❖ At this point there is no consideration of a "publication" in print. You are not going to type this up and distribute it.

❖ You are revising your OP by reading it aloud to yourself so that you can also read it aloud to an audience.

Reading what you have written out loud to yourself is not a new idea at all. Ira Shor made this point about reading out loud in "Monday Morning Fever: Critical Literacy and the Generative Theme of 'Work'":

> Voicing is a self-editing tool that calls on students to use the natural grammar in their speaking voices. The method is simple: after composing, you read out loud what you've written. The grammar in your speech will automatically correct errors made by your writing hand. All you have to do is carefully listen to your own voice as you read; wherever you stumble or hesitate, your strong speaking skills are being inter-

fered with by your less-developed writing skills. This development distinction between speech and encoding offers students a self-educating method that uses one of their strengths to remediate one of their weaknesses, without the learning activity passing through a teacher or grammar book.

(*Freire for the Classroom* 1987)

After students finish their revisions, they prepare a final copy (the copy they will hand in to us) that is easy for them to read. Then they practice reading to a pretend audience prior to their turns at the Formal Reading.

We set aside four or five days for the Formal Reading, and that usually allows for five readings each class period. Students sign up for the days they want to read. Also, we encourage our students to invite friends, family, other teachers, and administrators to the Formal Reading, sometimes for support and other times for a chance to impress them with some really good writing. Applause follows each reading, and once again discussion includes questions and comments from the audience focused on the content of the writing and not necessarily the style. By this point our students are comfortable reading aloud and directing discussion. There have been situations, though, when a student's writing has been emotionally difficult to get through, and we have stepped to the podium to help with a hug or even taking over the reading. Students hand in their Occasional Papers, and the teacher, after quickly checking for completion, assigns credit for a major grade of 100.

Grading Occasional Papers for a Class Book

Toward the end of a grading period, we often publish "class books." Each student in the class revises an OP, once again beginning with the reading out loud strategy and then ironing out mechanical and stylistic errors. One more point about revision: it is possible that in reading aloud, students can start to hear where there are problems to remedy. Maybe this kind of revision can apply to future pieces and the way students think about writing.

We cannot neglect to say that there is a competitive aspect in choosing an OP for the OP book. Students sometimes worry that the readers will overlook their OPs and just read what other students have written. There is motivation for students to want to write in a way that will make others want to read what they have written. If there was any confusion or misunderstanding of the OP when it was first read to the entire class, the discussion usually provided a clearer and fuller understanding. The writer could also notice that there was something needed that the paper did not provide. Because students are eager for other students to read their OPs, they don't necessarily write for praise from a teacher, but rather they write to communicate with their readers to demonstrate competencies.

After revising on their own, students can work in pairs or small groups to help each other proofread and polish their Occasional Papers. We gather the cleaned-up OPs, copy them, and then collate and staple together a very simple book. Distribution day is one of excitement – students look forward to passing around their class books for comments and autographs from classmates. Even though students focus on choosing and revising OPs for the class book that attract the attention of their classmates, they are responsible for proofreading their papers checking mechanics, including spelling and punctuation. We check to see if the OP's description of an experience and reflection are clear, coherent, organized, and complete, and assign a major grade for the class book assignment; deductions from 100 are for mechanical errors.

Grading Occasional Papers for a Writing Portfolio

Depending on the course, we require students to collect and to eventually turn in all of their writing in portfolios. This includes required writings and Occasional Papers. For example, in a Creative Writing elective, students write expository essays the first six weeks, short stories the second, and a collection of poetry the third. All this required writing is collected in their portfolios. We also assign students to write at least two Occasional Papers per six weeks and keep them in their portfolios. We teach students in composition courses at the college level, where they collect all required writings and Occasional Papers in portfolios. For instance, in one course, students write Summary Response Essays about literary and expository pieces they read throughout the semester. These essays become parts of their portfolios. Students also are assigned to write and read aloud to the class at least two Occasional Papers, and students collect them in their portfolios. Finally, we require our students to reflect about their writing – no matter the course - throughout the semester. After writing about a topic of choice in a Summary Response Essay, for example, a student will complete a Reflection about the writing experience.

In both the Creative Writing classes and the College Composition classes, Occasional Papers in open mic settings become a part of the curriculum using grading scale below.

Week One	1st OP 100	2nd OP 100
Week Two	1st OP 90	2nd OP 100
Week Three	1st OP 80	2nd OP 90
Week Four	1st OP 80	2nd OP 90
Week Five	1st OP 80	2nd OP 80
Week Six	1st OP 70	2nd OP 80

We have found the Occasional Paper assignment appeals to students not necessarily eager to write but with some prodding willing to write and read aloud their OPs in a non-threatening environment. Occasional Papers will likely give students new confidence in writing curriculum-required compositions, including the expository essay, the argumentative essay, the personal narrative, and the literary response essay. Students collect their writing (we hope all of it) in a portfolio. We provide this Reflection Sheet and Self-Evaluation Sheets for our students to complete and to assist us in our grading. We have assigned the Reflection Sheet and Self-Evaluation to students in our high school elective classes and students in freshman composition classes at the college level. The portfolio is a completion grade of 100; points are deducted for parts missing.

Reflection Sheet

1. What was especially important to you when you were writing this paper?

2. What do you see as the strengths in this piece of writing?

3. What did you have trouble with in writing this paper?

4. If you could work on this writing further, what would you do?

5. What were some of the reactions you received either from your teacher or from your peers about your paper?

Self-Evaluation Sheet (page 1)

Titles of required writings:

    1. _____ Reflection Sheet _____

    2. _____ Reflection Sheet _____

    3. _____ Reflection Sheet _____

Titles of required Occasional Papers:

    1. _____ Reflection Sheet _____

    2. _____ Reflection Sheet _____

Titles of additional OPs:

    1. _____ Reflection Sheet _____

    2. _____ Reflection Sheet _____

Self-Evaluation Sheet (page 2)

Learning:
This is not a content course in that we do not teach testable information. It is hoped that what you have learned are ways to go about reading and writing that suit you, that are BEST for you. Comment on what you have discovered about your own ways of reading and writing?

Support of the class:
Comment on your participation in discussion. How much effort did you put into contributing to discussion?

Talking:
One of the principles of this class is that we can learn from talking, both from talking with each other and exchanging ideas and also from "talking" our writing out loud, proofreading it by reading aloud, revising by reading aloud, and finding what we have to say by reading our own writing out loud. Comment on what you have learned about "learning by talking"?

UP-to Standard work
Did you in your best and most honest opinion do Up-to-Standard work in this course?

Did you in your best and most honest opinion do more work than what was necessary for Up-to-Standard performance?

Your turn:

If you tried one of the "destinations" in your classes, did it work? Write about whether or not it eased grading for you.

_____

_____

_____

If you haven't already, try the "reading it aloud to yourself" revising technique with students in any of your classes. What happened? Are you pleased with the results?

_____

_____

_____

Reflections:

Choose the answer that best describes what you think about each classroom "destination" and the stress-free grading that goes along with it.

1. How likely are you to try the open mic agenda with your students?

   ⑤ "very likely"   ④ "most likely"   ③ "Probably not likely"   ② "not likely"   ① "heck no"

2. How likely are you to do a formal reading with your students?

   ⑤ "very likely"   ④ "most likely"   ③ "Probably not likely"   ② "not likely"   ① "heck no"

3. How likely are you to put together a class book of Occasional Papers in any of your classes?

   ⑤ "very likely"   ④ "most likely"   ③ "Probably not likely"   ② "not likely"   ① "heck no"

4. How likely are you to require writing portfolios that include your students' required pieces of writing, required OPs, additional OPs, Reflection Sheets, and Self-Evaluation Sheets?

   ⑤ "very likely"   ④ "most likely"   ③ "Probably not likely"   ② "not likely"   ① "heck no"

Works Cited:

Applebee, Arthur N., Anne Auten, and Fran Lehr. *Writing in the Secondary School: English and the Content Areas*. Urbana, IL: National Council of Teachers of English, 1981. Print.

Dewey, John. *John Dewey: The Later Works*, 1925-1953, Vol. 8: 1933. Edited by JoAnn Boydston. Southern Illinois University Press, 1989.

Shor, Ira Ed. "Monday Morning Fever: Critical Literacy and the Generative Theme of 'Work.'" *Freire for the Classroom*: *A Sourcebook for Liberatory Teaching*. Heinemann Educational Books, Inc., 1987.

Chapter Nine

And Not Only That

Don't give up – give Occasional Papers a fair chance. Will your students' Occasional Papers be more work for you? No, not at all. Writing, reading aloud, and discussing Occasional Papers will free you up to really get to know your students. Eventually your OP classroom can become a writing community.

Throughout the chapters in *Teaching Writing in a Way That Students Embrace Enthusiastically,* we have tried to engage you in what it takes to create an Occasional Paper classroom. We begin chapters asking you where you are as teachers of writing, sharing what we do as teachers of writing, suggesting the Occasional Paper as a way for you to teach writing, challenging you with Your Turn activities, and asking you to reflect again at the end of each chapter. In this chapter we want to add the "not only that": our beliefs about student writing and discussion.

1. **We believe** practice in writing about issues of personal concern and practice with discussion behaviors will improve students' critical thinking, enrich their writing, and add to their ability to benefit from and contribute to citizenship in a democracy. And along with writing, will also make their lives better and make them better human beings.

2. **We believe** education is about making of meaning. Our most powerful tool for making meaning is language. We often think of schooling as focusing on reading and writing. Even though these are the evidence of the impact of language in the classroom, we need to acknowledge the importance of listening and speaking (including internal listening and speaking – i.e., thinking).

3. **We believe** the experience of others and a stance of inquiry about the meaning of our different experiences can be the foundation of good discussion and also can help us achieve a more ambitious goal: intellectual inquiry.

4. **We believe** students will learn how to talk reasonably, question each other civilly, and through the modeling of this interested and engaged talk, learn how to think about abstract ideas by relating them, not to other abstractions or to aphorisms, but to their own life experiences. This is good thinking, and it is the basis of, and is modeled by, good talk.

5. **We believe** radical curiosity obviously drives questioning. In normal conversation, questioning is constrained, and we ignore what is conventionally explicable. But inquiry is all about going beyond the conventional. Curiosity – radical curiosity – is the engine that drives inquiry and deep understanding.

6. **We believe** intellectual passion is the drive to really know, to really understand. It is the joy and satisfaction that come from understanding. It is the sometimes annoying persistence which will not be satisfied with less.

7. **We believe** a change in understanding is usually accomplished by the addition of new ideas, of new stories. A change in meaning is only accomplished when understanding opens new perspectives and new connections. It is changes in understanding that are the focus of successful discussion.

8. **We believe** our mission cannot simply be to prepare our students to continue their academic pursuits but must include preparing them for citizenship and for a rich and examined life. Discussion skills are perhaps the most important contribution education can make to preparing students for democratic citizenship and a richly examined life.

9. **We believe** for students to see themselves as real writers in the writing classroom, they have an opportunity to use their writing at the same time they observe and respond to the writing of their classmates. We want to build a writing community, a community which will motivate production, which will reward successful communication with understanding, and which will enhance the confidence and therefore the growth and experimentation of all the students in the class.

10. **We believe** Occasional Papers become more than a writing exercise and even more than a way to learn about inquiry, but they become a different way to go about self-education and a different way of experiencing life itself.

Finally, we both experienced having students who left at the end of the semester after spending many hours in talk and writing and reading their writing and listening to other students' ideas about the ideas they wrote about—after all of this they would leave saying something like "We might not have learned much about English, but we learned about life." We were horrified and didn't want them saying such things within earshot of the school administration or other teachers. Yes, we covered the curriculum along with Occasional Papers. But on the other hand, we felt successful in having at least started toward what we saw and still see as the goal of education: to learn about life, to learn about how to live. And of course, students will never leave at the end of the year saying, "Now I understand life!" with the same sense of accomplishment and mastery as they might leaving a science class saying, "Now I understand photosynthesis!" They will not even frame their understanding by saying "Now I know how to use language to find out about life" or "Now I know how to talk and read as a search for understanding."

But if they have learned to use language through talking and writing and reading and listening to better understand life—their lives—then we feel they are on the right track. This is engaged pedagogy, and it does not mean an abandonment of the traditional goals of academic work. But it does mean always thinking of traditional goals as markers or a bridge or a trail toward larger goals – "an unexamined life is not worth living" and all of that.

Resources

Bill was alerted that this testimony appeared on the MindBrainEd Think Tanks blog: What a wonderful surprise to learn about Julia Daley's love for and success with Occasional Papers in her teaching. The timing was perfect! We were about to publish our book and thrilled to add Julia's article to the Resources.

An Occasion for Students to Share

by Julia Daley

https://www.mindbrained.org/april-2022-outside-lives/

Back in my writing classes in the USA, this assignment was by far the most popular among my students. The idea was introduced to me by my department head and from the work of Bill Martin in his article "A Writing Assignment/A Way of Life" (2003) (https://www.jstor.org/stable/3650535); in his article, he introduces an assignment that he calls the "Occasional Paper" and shows how he uses it in his class to great effect. The premise is simple: students must prepare and share a piece of writing with the class. The topic is entirely up to them—be it something from their personal life (Martin's student shares about a game they played) or a topic they find interesting (no research necessary)—as is the timing of when they read it aloud to the class. It is not corrected in any way by the teacher; it's solely a completion grade. The "Occasional Paper" was a small part of my writing course, but it was instrumental in creating an open classroom atmosphere. I was repeatedly blown away by the pieces my students wrote and shared—their personal voices were readily apparent in their writing, in a way they rarely captured in other assignments. Each Occasional Paper revealed an aspect of my students' lives that I, and their classmates, hadn't known before.

To give a bit of context, the course was an introductory writing course for students at Northern Arizona University. It was a mandatory course that all students were expected to take and pass with a decent grade. Most students were freshmen, but I had the occasional sophomore, junior, senior, and even super senior. International students were expected to take the course as well, provided they had a high enough TOEFL score to take mainstream courses (and, if not, they took a sheltered version of the course run by the Program for Intensive English). Classes were not streamed—in one class, student ability levels could range from a non-native English speaker who'd never written more than a few sentences in English together, to students who were budding writers drafting novels in their free time. Over the 18-week semester, the students were responsible for writing six essays with two revisions each, as well as one "Occasional Paper."

I always introduced the "Occasional Paper" to students on the very first day of the course, with these guidelines:

> 1) Any topic is okay.
>   *provided it is school-appropriate, and you are comfortable sharing it with the entire class*
>
> 2) It cannot be an assignment used for any other course.
>
> 3) It must be between 350 ~ 500 words.
>
> 4) It must be written on a piece of paper (typed or handwritten).
>
> 5) It must be read aloud in class by XX date.

I tweaked my guidelines a bit from those suggested by Bill Martin. These are what worked best with my students, but they can easily be changed for different contexts. This is so that there's enough text that it'll take students between 3 to 5 minutes to read aloud. With lower-level ELL students, this word count can be reduced. This is to make sure the students did take time to actually write something down. I usually chose a point midway through the semester, at about the 8-week mark.

I followed the assignment introduction by reading my own "Occasional Paper" as a model for students (my piece on my experience being bullied on a school bus was always a hit with my students). I found the modeling to be important: the piece I shared usually set the tone for my students. If I shared something a bit personal, my students were more likely to follow suit with their own papers. Students were encouraged to talk to me before class and let me know if they had an "Occasional Paper" to share that day. I always tried to leave room in my lesson plans for 1-2 papers from students, or about 5-10 minutes of time. If I was lucky, I'd have an eager student ready to share an "Occasional Paper" within the first week of class (most memorable was a Super Senior who shared hers the second day of class, an excellent piece with lots of advice she wished she had known as a first-year student). But if I hadn't gotten a volunteer after the first week of class, I'd start nudging some of the more gregarious students to prepare something. The absolute freedom in topic could be paralyzing for my students, as, for many of them, this was the first time they'd had the chance to write about anything they wanted. I'd eavesdrop on chatting students, and suggest "Wow, that'd make a great 'Occasional Paper!'" to help give them some ideas. Once the first couple of students had gone, I found I'd get a nice flow of 3-5 volunteers each week.

I absolutely love this assignment, and it made a huge difference in the relationships my students had with each other. Many students would share something personal about their lives and would receive positive feedback and comments from their peers (and sometimes some great discussions, as time allowed). Even though I did not correct any grammar in the "Occasional Papers," I did collect the papers from the students once they were finished reading. I always made sure to leave some positive comments thanking the students for sharing about themselves before returning their "Occasional Papers." Years later, I still fondly remember many of the stories my students shared. Some of the greatest hits included: two students in the same class sharing two different stories about their cars catching on fire; a Saudi student sharing a hilarious piece on following a woman around in a supermarket that he thought was his mother; a politically active student chronicling his experience at a Donald Trump rally during the 2016 election campaign, and more.

The "Occasional Paper" became such a popular assignment that I would frequently have students ask if they could share a second or third one. I caved to their demands and made an extra credit "Occasional Paper" assignment for the second half of the semester. Students always looked forward to when their peers would share an "Occasional Paper"—there would usually be chatter before class as the students would ask each other if anyone had written something for the day.

In my course evaluations, students wrote that this assignment was the first time they enjoyed writing because they didn't have to worry about errors or formatting; they could just write whatever they wanted. If you're looking for a creative yet productive way for students to share something about themselves, you can't go wrong with bringing the "Occasional Paper" into your classroom.

> *Julia Daley is a lecturer at Hiroshima Bunkyo University, where she teaches English conversation and writing. She earned her MA in TESL at Northern Arizona University and is certified to teach secondary English in Arizona. She appreciates everyone's patience as she's been learning how to build a* website.

Daley, J. *MindBrainEd Think Tanks: Why Language Teachers Should Know about Their Learners' Lives Outside the Classroom.* Vol. 8, 2022, pp. 20–23.

Discussion Guides

When your students begin to write Occasional Papers, you may find discussions uncomfortable for yourself and them. You might find these three discussion guides or "cheat sheets" helpful. The guides provide examples of how a teacher can enter into a discussion by first affirming previous comments and then suggesting alternate routes the discussion can take.

The Directions a Discussion Can Go

Same level of generality:

> You talked about trouble training your cocker spaniel; I had trouble training my cocker spaniel also.

Up and down the ladder: From incident to general statement and from general statement to example and from chaos to patterns.

> <u>Up</u>: You talked about trouble training your cocker spaniel. Are cocker spaniels in general difficult to train?

> <u>Down</u>: You talked about training your cocker spaniel. At what point in the training did you first experience difficulty?

Looking and looking again: This seems to be what we are considering but is that really it? Is that really an accurate description or formulation?

> You talk about trouble training your cocker spaniel. I'm wondering if what you call trouble is just a normal part of the training process.

Stepping closer: Can you say more about that? How did it feel? What did you think? What effect has it had?

> You talk about trouble training your cocker spaniel. Can you say something about how this felt? Did it have an effect on how you felt (or feel) about the dog?

Changing the lens: Can we see this from a different person's perspective or from the standpoint of a different theoretical frame?

> You talk about trouble training your cocker spaniel. I'd like to consider when training is directed at natural dog behaviors and when it is directed at unnatural dog behaviors.

Backing away: How is this unit of experience affected by time? How is it related to its context? How is it determined by the culture?

> You talk about trouble training your cocker spaniel. Did the trouble lead to eventual success? When did you do and where did you do the training? Where do your ideas about how a good dog should behave come from?

Questions to Ask During Discussion

You can open up a discussion by asking students to elaborate on and explore ideas they have shared.

What does this have to do with me, with us?

> What do we train (tame) other than dogs? In other words, are there ways in which we are all involved in training something in some way?

What's an analogy?

> How is training a dog like installing an irrigation system?

Has this happened before? Will it happen again? How will it be different?

> Does training a dog always mean the same thing? What else could it mean?

What's affected by this happening?

> How much does this improve the owner's life? How much does it improve the dog's life?

What's a commonplace saying, a maxim, that connects with this? What about the maxim doesn't fit?

> Does this come from the same parenting attitude that "children should be seen and not heard"?

What misunderstandings are most likely when you tell someone something like this?

> Do you even really want a dog? What do you love about your dog? Would you be happier with an animal like a bird that stayed in a cage?

Did this incident depend on something (or some things) that happened prior to this happening?

Have you trained other dogs? Is this different from other "more successful" experiences you've had with dog training?

Upping the Ante for Discussion

Teachers can use these activities to push a discussion to a higher level of inquiry.

Time Out to Write: Do one or two minutes of freewriting to collect thoughts and assess gaps and confusions. Topic of the writing could be "What do I have to say about this?" or "What questions do I have about this topic?"

Consult with a Partner: Briefly talk with a person sitting next to you about the topic being discussed. Ask the partner if your question or comment seems like a good one. Maybe the two of you can revise it or refocus it.

Designated Respondents: Choose two students (or have the reader of the paper choose two students) to be the designated respondents who will have questions ready to start the discussion after the paper has been read. Other questions come after the two designated respondents have performed their obligation.

Instant Poll Taking: Ask about experiences related to this topic. "How many of you have ever . . .?" "How many of you think . . .?" Follow up with a question for an individual to answer "Who has something to say about your own experience?"

Ready-Made Starters: Challenge students to think of a question starting with a particular question word. "Who can think of a question we could ask that starts with 'Who'?" Other starter words: Why, Where, When, etc. Starting phrases: "Is there a difference . . .?" "Do you think that . . . ?" "Do you mean . . . ?"

Tag Team Summary Response: Ask students to think of anything they remember the author saying. (Of course, this can lead to trivial details, but the process is the important thing, so just relax about the level of complexity.) Student A offers a comment the author made. Then ask if anyone can think of a question to ask about this point. This is summary / response question format, but it is broken up into two parts: one student contributes the "you said" part and a second student contributes the "my question is" part.

Parallel Experience: Ask students if anyone has had a parallel experience. The follow-up discussion is an investigation of how the parallel experience is different from the author's experience and what difference this makes.

Variations for Including Occasional Papers in Established Curriculums

Not only have we asked students to write Occasional Papers (OPs) in our **High School English** classes and **College Composition** classes, but we have also included Occasional Papers in our elective curriculums. For example, we taught **Creative Writing** and **Visual Media** electives and included OPs as a writing and class discussion experience.

If you decide to include Occasional Papers in any of your courses, you should consider the following questions:

✓ **How many Occasional Papers do you want to require during a grading period?** OPs are papers read aloud to the class, discussed by the class, handed in, and graded for completion. To earn a 100, the paper must include a title, the description of an experience, and a reflection about the experience. We have usually required one or two OPs during a grading period.

✓ **How much time do you want to take in introducing OPs to your students?** Do you want your students to read their first Occasional Papers aloud in pairs or small groups? Or, skipping pair and small group sharing, do you want students to read aloud complete OPs to the entire class and discuss them with their classmates?

✓ **Can you see the following framework working in your classes?** If you read the article about using Occasional Papers in a **Creative Writing** class, you'll see the first six weeks of the course is based on the Occasional Paper and ends with polishing one OP to be used as personal narrative. While students focus on poetry the second six weeks and focus on short stories the third six weeks, two OPs are required per grading period, using the open mic agenda for reading OPs aloud and discussing them.

✓ **Is this option a possibility for you?** If you're teaching a **Writing Skills** class, or any other elective with a focus on writing, you could spend several weeks teaching the Occasional Paper, having your students share their writing first with a partner, then in small groups, and eventually in front of the class. Your students' OPs would be the main writing assignment during the grading period.

✓ **Will the open mic agenda work in your classes?** This involves students reading aloud and discussing their OPs at the beginning of the class period any day of the week. On the other hand, you could reserve OP readings for certain days of the week, for example, Monday, Wednesday, and Friday *or* Tuesday and Thursday, *or* Friday only. What option is best for you?

Finally, reading Occasional Papers at the end of the class period can limit time for discussion which will take away from the entire OP experience - missing feedback to the writer and the opportunity for inquiry by all members of the class. We believe the reading of OPs as a "filler" activity at the end of a class period "demotes" the value of the Occasional Paper assignment.

Sample Occasional Papers

When I Wake Up

Dear Martin and fellow friends and classmates,

When I wake up, I will feel an emptiness in my heart. When I think about this class, I feel sad. I have had the best semester ever in college. For the first time in forever, I felt that I could express my thoughts and my feelings. I felt that I didn't have to feel shy or embarrassed about my OPs and essays.

I have learned a lot in this class and have also learned something new about y'all. I wish this class would never end; I have made most of you my friends. Now that we're only one day away from the semester ending, I feel really sad, and there is an emptiness in my heart. Now when I wake up, I won't be in a hurry to drive to school and beat the traffic. Now when I wake up, I'll feel lost not knowing what to do. I might end up going to work, but even that won't make me forget about my class. The memories we make today and tomorrow will be the only things that last, and the memories I will cherish for the rest of my life. I just want to thank you for always listening and not judging. I found a friendship with each and every one of you.

Now we all have to choose our paths whether they are good or bad. To get a future and better ourselves. I wish you all the best from the bottom of my heart and will always remember you with a smile. When I wake up from this great dream of my class…

Written at the end of a semester, this letter is mainly a reflection of the
student's appreciation and sadness when she no longer attends this class.

Saving Animals

While I was taking care of my baby brother one Saturday afternoon, I was changing the channels to put a cartoon on for him when this commercial came on about mistreated animals. I watched the whole video, I couldn't hold my tears, when I realized that no animal, and no human should be treated wrong.

I also realized that I need to go out there and make a difference by helping animals in need. I have a dog as well and throughout time I loved her even more. Animals are special and they need our help to survive in this world. That day changed my life and my thoughts about animals. My dog's warmth and love keep me on track of achieving my goal to be a veterinarian.

This OP has the traditional structure: experience followed by reflection.

The Father I Never Had

Sometimes it doesn't matter how hard you try or how much you want things to work, sometimes it's not meant to be. I guess all is destiny.

My father broke my heart…killed what was left of my love and trust for him. I've always understood he had a problem with alcohol since I remember. But how can I love a father that has never been there for me? How can I love a man that never earned the word father? A father that didn't raise us and take care of us when we needed him. My mother earned the word father thanks to her love and support that have helped me in life, and I am still here trying so hard to have a career.

This weekend I realized my father doesn't love me or my brother. We got a call saying he was sick in the hospital. It was a hard decision, but we decided to see him and a couple of his family members that are no longer my family. They insulted us, and my father didn't defend us or say anything. In fact, he told us to leave so we did. That night I said to myself that no matter in what condition he is, I will no longer go see him.

I lost my father a long time ago. Now I just know that that man has a lot of anger and bitterness in his heart that only thinks of the past. A man that has only tried to infect us with hate. Right now I am trying to move on, let it go, and not let hate grow in my heart towards the father that I once had.

The writer chose to write a reflection first, followed by a description of an experience. Plus, including a large amount of reflection is certainly okay.

Improving Me

I want to improve myself in every aspect of my life. I feel like I've been a lazy bum throughout my whole life, and so far, it hasn't gotten me anywhere, and that needs to change since I have many goals that I want to accomplish.

My first goal is to get myself any sort of college certificate and move on to a four-year institution which hopefully will be UT. It is located in the best city in the world which is Austin, and I don't see myself leaving anytime soon. My other very important goal is to open up my own restaurant with my dad. He's been working in a kitchen for many years, and he loves what he does. Owning a successful restaurant has been one of his life-long dreams, and I really want to help him fulfill his dream. And lastly my most desired goal is to try out for a professional soccer team before I turn 21 to see what I'm capable of and chase my life-long goal of becoming a professional soccer player.

In order to accomplish any of these goals, I will need to work hard and be committed to everything I do. To get a college certificate and transfer to UT, I will need to get good grades. To open the restaurant with my dad I will need to have money and have some sort of business administration experience. To be able to go to a tryout for a soccer team, I will need to lose weight and get fit. For that to happen, I need to start eating right and exercising more often. While sometimes I slack off and do things without any motivation, I always have my goals stuck in my head that I envision one day will become a reality.

This OP has a nice intro that leads into a paragraph describing various experiences. The third paragraph is reflective about those experiences.

Different Lives

Like any other day I'm at work cashiering. So many people come through my line every day and to be honest it's very interesting to be "kinda" a part of someone else's life for 3 to 5 minutes. To see the different personalities and lifestyles is very interesting. For example, the way the kids act with their parents or how the parents are with other adults is very interesting.

So, a customer came through my line, and she had kids. These kids were yelling and standing there looking at the groceries not being packed. We then finished the order, and the parent customer and I went to bag the items. She told her kids to move over to she could bag. Let me just say that if I was with my dad or even my mom, I would for sure be bagging and helping.

It's so weird to me that so many people are different with different personalities and different standards. My family and I never talk about having anxiety or being depressed. We look at the positive and believe everything is possible. We honestly don't understand people who have anxiety, depression, or suicidal thoughts. It's not that we don't believe that people are affected that way. We just don't personally go through what other people to. As to what I was saying, people are just so different from one another.

This OP begins with a reflection and then the description of the experience. The beginning of last paragraph has a nice transition, but then the reflection takes a leap and does not relate back to the cashiering experience.

A Creative Writing Class Starts with Occasional Papers

by Christine Gorychka

My principal asked me to design and teach a one-semester creative writing class open to all students in grades 9 - 12. There were no prerequisites, a limited number of objectives in the state curriculum guide, and no state-mandated standardized test at the end of the semester. So, I had the freedom and the fun of putting together a course for writers with different interests, motivations, and abilities. Also, I counseled with Bill along the way as I built a creative writing program. A wide variety of students signed up for the first Creative Writing I class, from ninth graders who needed extra writing practice to upperclassmen who enjoyed writing and looked forward to exploring different writing avenues.

As I developed an outline for the course and began building lessons, I thought the best and quickest way to build a community of writers was to begin the semester with Occasional Papers (OPs). In his article "Real-World Writing: Making Purpose and Audience Matter," Grant Wiggins sums up perfectly what Occasional Papers can do. He claims that "the point of writing is to have something to say and make a difference in saying it" (29). Because my students would write about topics of their choice, they should have something to say and make a difference just by reading their writing out loud and discussing their papers with their peers. In my English classes, students loved writing and hearing OPs, so the Occasional Paper assignment surely would work in a creative writing class. And it did.

In the following set of lesson plans, the semester is divided into three 6-week periods. Weeks 1 and 2 of the first 6-week grading period are described in detail, followed by summaries of the remaining 4 weeks. Then I briefly describe the focus of the second and third 6-week grading periods. If your semester has four 9-week grading periods, you easily can adjust activities and modify this schedule.

First six weeks of the Fall semester

Week 1:

Monday: To begin, I asked my students to write a couple of sentences about themselves that they would willingly read aloud to the class. We wrote for five minutes and everyone, including me, read our sentences aloud and applauded after each reading. We ended the class period talking about the importance of reading OPs out loud to the class followed by applause. Increasing the comfort level of my students was a goal the first day of class, and thankfully this ice breaker met little resistance, plus students learned a little about one another.

Tuesday: After sentence sharing on Monday, I explained we would take the first steps in writing an "Occasional Paper." Like Nancie Atwell, I believed that "getting everyone started writing on a topic of his or her choosing is the main thing to accomplish the first day of school" (76). So on the second day of class I read aloud a description about a recent experience of mine to start the ball rolling:

I walked out on my porch this morning, and a small brown and orange bird darted out of a pretty flowering plant next to the door. Curious, I looked inside the plant, and toward the back was the beginning of a nest – a collection of leaves, small twigs, wilted flowers, and tufts of dog hair. My husband and I had been on vacation the week before, and I'm betting the nest-building began then.

A nice surprise … my students remembered to applaud! Then they asked questions and commented about my description, and they also volunteered similar experiences. Our discussion focused on content and not necessarily writing style. I explained that their assignment for Wednesday was to write a 150–200-word description of an experience or realization of their own choosing, possibly something that happened to them in the last 24 hours. We ended that class period brainstorming topic ideas:

- ❖ Even though I say I'm going to sleep seven to eight hours every night, it never happens.

- ❖ I watched the cooking channel last night and decided to try making Beef Wellington with my grandmother.

- ❖ With a long trip a week away, I look at the table of "stuff" I have to pack, yawn, and decide to take a nap before digging in.

- ❖ Last week I had to put my dog to sleep. It was so hard to say good-bye to my friend. How I miss him.

Wednesday: To begin the class period, students read what they had written to a partner, once again focusing on questions for the reader and the sharing of similar experiences after each reading. Then I explained that an Occasional Paper or "OP" includes both the description of an experience and a reflection about that experience. I read my description aloud again, this time adding a reflection:

I walked out on my porch this morning, and a small brown and orange bird darted out of a pretty flowering plant next to the door. Curious, I looked inside the plant and toward the back was the beginning of a nest – a collection of leaves, small twigs, wilted flowers, and tufts of dog hair. My husband and I had been on vacation the week before, and I was betting the nest-building began then.

Would baby birds hatch and then practice their flying soon? I was so excited about that possibility because I had never experienced anything like that in my life. I had never seen puppies or kittens born, let alone baby birds hatch. I kept checking on the nest and figured the mother and father must sit on the eggs all night, because each morning as I opened the door to the porch, out they darted to gather seed and other food. So, a waiting game began. I waited for days, then a week, then two, and finally two little birds flew out of the plant, fluttering their wings and sometimes tumbling to the porch floor, getting their bearings and flying back to their nest. After much encouragement from Mom and Dad, plus practice, the two little birds were on their own, and flew away from home. I began to think about how in such a short time, two newly hatched birds learned to fly and then independently flew away.

Reflecting the years it took my two children to grow into their independence and the process: steps like going to an overnight camp, spending time away from home with grandparents and friends, learning to do their own laundry, the list goes on. Finally they left home for college, and their worlds changed.

There had to be times of fear, loneliness, and dread for my kids in their new college worlds. They had to get used to living with new roommates, being a little homesick once in a while, getting themselves to class on their own, choosing a major, engaging with their professors, reading and studying new material and preparing for tests, maintaining a decent grade-point, learning the ropes in a brand-new social world, and staying within their budgets. My kids evolved into college students who journeyed down new roads of learning and eventually earned bachelor's degrees, new jobs, and incomes. Like the baby birds, my children left their nests and flew into new worlds.

Students again applauded, asked questions, and shared similar experiences and reflections. My finished OP was probably over the top in length, but admittedly, I couldn't stop writing. Watching the baby birds learn to fly and leave the nest for good added more detail to the "description of an experience" portion of my OP, plus my "reflection" was fairly long and a bit philosophical. I think it was okay for my students to realize that Occasional Papers were not short journal writings but essays with some length and depth.

In case some students were not catching on to what it meant to reflect, we practiced by filling in this sentence together:

After I _____, I felt like _____.

For example, *After I watched two baby bird learn to fly and leave their nest, I realized that my two children learned "to fly" to new worlds of independence.*

Each student completed the sentence above, and volunteers read theirs aloud for the rest of the class. Then I assigned a 250 – 350-word Occasional Paper (OP #1) that followed the recipe below for Thursday's class. I also reminded students to type or write out their OPs, title them, and focus on the content of their writing, not necessarily worrying about manuscript correctness.

1	Be on the lookout for a moment or an experience that makes you stop and think.
2	Describe the moment or experience in writing.
3	Add a reflection about its significance. Why does it matter to you? What meaning can you give it?
4	Read your OP aloud to an audience, probably a small group or our entire class.
5	Respond to audience questions and comments about the content of your OP.

Thursday: Class opened with students reading their OPs to partners, followed by discussion: questions and comments for the writer and the sharing of similar situations. Then I explained that on Friday each one of them would read their first Occasional Papers in writing groups of four students. Since most of the students in the class did not know each other very well, and in order for them to get the hang of the reading aloud and the discussion elements of the OP assignment, we began with small groups. All would share the OPs they had been working on or write brand new ones. Besides writing a description of an experience and a reflection about that experience, each OP had to have a descriptive title and be typed or handwritten.

Friday: In class together for less than a week, I randomly assigned my students to writing groups, mixing grade levels and boys and girls. They followed the same process in reading and sharing their OPs as they did when working with their partners. Also, as they listened to an OP, they filled out the form below and shared their reactions with each other:

Writing Group Response Form

OP # 1	OP # 1	OP # 1
Author: Chris Gorychka Title: Flight	Author: Title:	Author: Title:
Does the OP have a description of an experience? Yes	Does the OP have a description of an experience?	Does the OP have a description of an experience?
Does the OP have a reflection of an experience? Yes	Does the OP have a reflection of an experience?	Does the OP have a reflection of an experience?
I have these questions about the OP: What kind of birds?	I have these questions about the OP:	I have these questions about the OP:
I have had similar experiences: I rescued an injured bird.	I have had similar experiences:	I have had similar experiences:

At the end of the class period, students handed in their Occasional Papers and response forms. I looked over the OPs for titles, descriptions of experiences, and reflections, and I also checked the response forms for serious comments and questions.

Week 2

Monday: I handed back last week's OPs and response forms. After reviewing the format for an OP - a description of an experience followed by a reflection - I explained that a variation could be writing the reflection first and then adding the description of the experience. Also, the reflection could be interspersed throughout the description of an experience. I read aloud a personal essay from our school's creative arts magazine that illustrated the components in an Occasional Paper: experience and reflection. This essay began with a reflective tribute to a parent who had recently died, then told the back story of experiences the writer had shared with his dad and ended with a lengthy reflection about the writer's relationship with his father through the years, circling back to present time and the current celebration of his father's life. I asked my students to write their next Occasional Papers (OP #2) keeping the personal essay in mind along with the variations in organizing their papers.

We brainstormed topic ideas and ended the class period with a 5-minute free write about an idea for OP #2.

❖ My mother sent me to the grocery store for a can of tomato sauce. I searched and searched and decided tomato paste had to be the same thing. Boy was I wrong!

❖ My friends and I went to the movie *Wicked* because we had heard it was really good and based on *The Wizard of Oz*. About 30 minutes into the show I fell asleep and wanted my money back.

❖ I couldn't figure out why my cousin wouldn't call me back.

❖ One more college application to go. Now the waiting begins.

Tuesday: Students spent the class period working on the first drafts of their second OPs that were to be 350-400 words long and due Wednesday. The final draft was due Friday for sharing in their writing groups.

Wednesday: Students read their first drafts to their partners and discussed the content of the OPs and similar experiences.

Thursday: To demonstrate to my students how their writing groups should work, we watched a video of four high school students sharing their writing. To begin, a writer read a piece of writing twice. The first time through others in the group just listened, and then during the second reading, listeners wrote down notes and shared their reactions with the writer. Finally, as the writer listened to comments and questions, she jotted down notes on her paper with the understanding that in the end, the writer decided what advice to follow, what suggested changes to make to the writing.

Friday: I assigned four students to each writing group, again considering grade level, gender, and writing maturity. Students followed the protocol demonstrated in yesterday's video and filled out the form below. They listened to each OP once, then during the second reading wrote notes on the response form. Each author noted what members of the writing group had to say and jotted those suggestions on her OP. At the end of the class period, students handed in their second Occasional Papers along with the completed form, and I looked over their papers for a completion grade.

Writing Group Response Form

OP # 2	OP # 2	OP # 2
Author: Title:	Author: Title:	Author: Title:
What I liked about the OP:	What I liked about the OP:	What I liked about the OP:
What I didn't understand:	What I didn't understand:	What I didn't understand:
Suggestions I have for the writer:	Suggestions I have for the writer:	Suggestions I have for the writer:

Week 3

At the beginning of the third week of the six weeks, I told my students that the assignment for the week was a third Occasional Paper (OP #3) of 500 words, and next week one of their three OPs would be polished in order to be used as a personal essay. Also, I thought it was time to let them know that during week 5, each one of them would read a personal essay aloud to the class at a "Formal Reading" in the Fine Arts theater. In addition to giving the students time to work with partners in preparation for writing groups on Friday, I also read aloud to them throughout the week personal essays by professional writers, including Annie Dillard, Bill Bryson, Marion Winik, Ellen DeGeneres, and Garrison Keillor. We talked about each essay's description of an experience, reflection about the experience, and the author's voice, especially the consistency of a certain tone. Did the essay have, for example, a humorous or sarcastic tone? Or was the tone more serious, possibly one of regret or embarrassment? In addition to focusing on detailed description and thoughtful reflection, I challenged students to write with a consistent tone.

We also spent some time during the week practicing sentence combining, vocabulary, and elaboration exercises.

Students met in their same writing groups on Friday to read aloud and discuss their third Occasional Papers just as they had the week before. Each of them completed the form below and handed it in with their OPs for my quick check and completion grade.

Writing Group Response Form

OP # 3 Author: Title:	OP # 3 Author: Title:	OP # 3 Author: Title:
What I liked about the OP:	What I liked about the OP:	What I liked about the OP:
What I didn't understand:	What I didn't understand:	What I didn't understand:
Suggestions I have for the writer:	Suggestions I have for the writer:	Suggestions I have for the writer:

Week 4

This week students chose an Occasional Paper to polish into a personal essay for the Formal Reading. They worked in class on their essays and conferenced with partners and with me. Also, throughout the week I read essays by professional writers and discussed with the class the authors' descriptions of experiences and reflections.

Dreams from My Father by Barack Obama

Sixteen Pictures of My Father by Marion Winik

The Woman Warrior: Memoirs of a Girlhood Among Ghosts by Maxine Hong Kingston

The Liars' Club by Mary Karr

Growing Up by Russell Baker

The Backyard Bird Chronicles by Amy Tan

Writers on Writing: Collected Essays from The New York Times

We also brainstormed topic ideas, keeping in mind to be on the lookout for a moment or an experience that makes you stop and think. Below are a few suggestions.

- ❖ For breakfast this morning, should I have peanut butter toast or take the time to make my favorite eggs benedict?

- ❖ It's getting to be cost prohibitive to buy tickets for a concert or a sporting event.

- ❖ I'm wondering if it's good for any dog breed to "manufacture" a doodle, for example the golden doodle or the labradoodle.

- ❖ When my parents told me about their divorce, I was devastated.

- ❖ I love to water ski and would love to learn how to snow ski.

We also talked about using figurative language, showing rather than telling, and considering different patterns of organization. Students signed up when to read the next week at the Formal Reading.

Week 5

The class met the entire week in a small theater in the fine arts building. Students stood at the podium to read a typed or hand-written copies of their personal essays. We usually ended up with about five readings per day. The audience applauded after each reading, and the writer then called on students with raised hands who had questions and comments. I kept a tally of audience responses; each student was required to comment or question at least five times during the week to earn a 100 grade. I encouraged my students to invite guests to the Formal Reading, for example, their parents, other teachers, administrators at the high school, friends who were available. We usually had a couple of guests each day. As a first, the Formal Reading was a success: readings and discussions ran smoothly, and comments and questions were heartfelt and honest. I remember rescuing a writer once in a while with a hug of encouragement or finishing up the reading aloud myself.

Week 6

During the last week of the grading period students revised, edited, and typed their personal essays for publication in a class book. While considering the feedback from last week's formal reading, each student understood that as the writer, he could choose which suggestions to consider and which suggestions to ignore. There was also the option to write a new Occasional Paper or polish either OP #1 or OP #2. Students conferenced with their partners and me, focusing on both content and manuscript correctness. We created a class book that included everyone's writing, and I distributed a copy to everyone in the class. That, too, was a really special day with students autographing each other's books and reading personal essays, new Occasional Papers, and even OPs they had heard before. Students were also required to submit a piece of writing to our high school's creative arts magazine for possible publication or send the writing to any other magazine or writing contest.

Grading

Because Creative Writing was an elective, I was not expected, nor did I want to assign grades to my students' pieces of writing like I would in a grade-level English or AP English class. I based grades for the most part on completion and a collection of points, somewhat like a pass/fail system with deductions for missing parts.

OP #1	100 points	for 200 - 300 words

5-point deduction for lack of length, experience, reflection, title
100 points for writing workshop form, -5 deduction for missing parts

OP #2	100 points	for 350 - 400 words

5-point deduction for lack of length, experience, reflection, title
100 points for writing workshop form, -5 deduction for missing parts

OP #3	100 points	for 500+ words

5-point deduction for lack of length, experience, reflection, title
100 points for writing workshop form, -5 deduction for missing parts

Formal Reading	200 points	for reading to our class a personal essay of at least 500 words

5-point deduction for lack of length, experience, reflection, title, consistent tone
Formal Reading Response Tally: 5 comments/questions =100 points
20-point deduction per missing comment/question

Class Book Submission	100 points

5-point deduction per manuscript error

Other Publication Submission	100 points

5-point deduction per manuscript error

Practice Writing Activities	100 points

5-point deduction for missing parts

The rest of the semester

During the **Second Six Weeks** the class focused on poetry, and then the **Third Six Weeks** students wrote short stories. Also, during the two remaining grading periods of the semester, I required students to write and read aloud to the class two OPs written outside of class to earn the 100 points for each. So that students would not wait until the end of the grading period to write and read OPs, I lessoned the point value per OP during week 3 and week 4 to 80 points. I used the same grading system discussed in Chapter 8.

Week One	1st OP 100	2nd OP 100
Week Two	1st OP 90	2nd OP 100
Week Three	1st OP 80	2nd OP 90
Week Four	1st OP 80	2nd OP 90
Week Five	1st OP 80	2nd OP 80
Week Six	1st OP 70	2nd OP 80

Throughout the rest of the semester, the students set their own agendas with the open mic system. We began each class period with my call for OP readings: "Does anyone have an Occasional Paper to read to our class today?" Sometimes there were none and other times quite a few. Very often the OPs were responses to other students' OPs which invited interesting discussion. I believe our Occasional Paper assignment contributed to building a community of writers more than any other assignment I could have given to my students. I also think that thanks to Occasional Papers, my students became more confident writers and, in many cases, more accomplished writers who easily transitioned into writing personal essays, poetry, and short stories.

Although I experienced moments of frustration and anxiety – quickly calling an end to inappropriate language, heart-to-hearts with cynical critics who thought they knew everything there was to know about everyone else's writing, and personal stories so heart-wrenching we all cried - the class model that included Occasional Papers held and expanded into more sections. A few years later a Creative Writing II course filled the second semester with a focus on personal essay, poetry, and screen plays. That class also read submissions and selected pieces for the fine arts magazine, *The Final Draft*. Occasional papers continued to prevail in both courses, semester after semester. My students loved them, asked for them, and one student even wrote an OP about his dream of OP banners flying across the sky. What a tribute to a writing assignment that worked.

Works Cited:
Atwell, Nancie. *In the Middle: Writing, Reading, and Learning with Adolescents*. Portsmouth, NH: Heinemann. 1987.

Wiggins, Grant. "Real-world Writing: Making Purpose and Audience matter." *English Journal*. Vol. 98.5, 2009, pp. 29-37.

Authors

Bill Martin earned his Ph.D. in linguistics from the University of Texas, an M.A. from the University of Kentucky in English Education, and a B.A. in English with honors from Oberlin College. After serving in the Peace Corp and teaching two years at the Orme School in Mayer, AZ, Bill began his 35-year teaching career in Austin, TX. As department chair at Hill Country Middle School and, later, at Westlake High School in Eanes ISD, Bill led his departments in NEH Summer Seminars and National Writing Project workshops. He also was selected to present sessions at National Council of Teachers of English (NCTE) national conferences as well as conferences of the Texas Council of Teachers of English Language Arts (TCTELA). Through the years Bill remained current in professional literature in the field of English education and published over 30 articles on composition, frequently in the *English Journal* and NCTE affiliate journals. In 2015, he was selected high school teacher of the year at Westlake High School. Along with Chris, Bill developed a curriculum around the use of Occasional Papers.

Christine Gorychka earned an M.A. from the University of Texas at Austin in Curriculum and Instruction and a B.S. in English Education at Iowa State University. Passionate about teaching, Chris taught 31 years in secondary English classrooms in Pflugerville ISD and Eanes ISD. She also chaired the English departments at Pflugerville High School and Westlake High School (WHS) and built a Creative Writing program at WHS. Interested in teaching other teachers, Chris presented professional development sessions at NCTE and TCTELA, and at Advanced Placement weekend conferences and Summer Institutes. Elected Teacher of the Year at WHS and ready to retire, Chris joined the College Board to organize and oversee AP conferences and to service school districts with College Board programs. 10 years later she filled a position at the Institute of Public School Initiatives (IPSI) at the University of Texas. As a Project Manager, she oversaw the production of secondary online English lessons, many written by Bill, for The Texas Education Agency's Project Share.

Although they taught different courses at Westlake High School, Chris and Bill built their writing programs around the Occasional Paper or OP, and through the years they continued to revise, rethink, and improve the use of OPs. Also, together, they published articles about Occasional Papers and shared their OP experiences at local, state, and national conferences. All culminated in the writing of *Teaching Writing in a Way That Students Embrace Enthusiastically*. This book for teachers promotes the Occasional Paper as an ongoing classroom activity, a writing practice (not a one-shot assignment) that builds writing skills and critical thinking skills, and which shapes students into writers who actually think of themselves as writers. Ultimately, this book shares an authority-grounded writing sequence based on Occasional Papers that can work as the backbone of any writing program.

We welcome your questions and comments.

You can reach Bill at coachbob@icloud.com and Chris at cgorychka@gmail.com.

www.ingramcontent.com/pod-product-compliance
Lightning Source LLC
Chambersburg PA
CBHW081002120626
46546CB00010B/2996

* 9 7 8 1 9 5 9 6 0 0 0 9 1 *